Constitutional
Amendments

From Freedom of Speech to Flag Burning

Volume 3:
Amendments 18-26, and the Unratified Amendments

Tom Pendergast, Sara Pendergast, and John Sousanis
Elizabeth Shaw Grunow, Editor

AN IMPRINT OF THE GALE GROUP

DETROIT · NEW YORK · SAN FRANCISCO
LONDON · BOSTON · WOODBRIDGE, CT

Constitutional Amendments
From Freedom of Speech to Flag Burning

Tom Pendergast
Sara Pendergast
John Sousanis

Staff

Elizabeth Shaw Grunow, U·X·L Editor
Carol DeKane Nagel, U·X·L Managing Editor
Thomas L. Romig, U·X·L Publisher

Elizabeth Des Chenes, Richard Clay Hanes, Kris E. Palmer, Contributing Editors

Julie Juengling, Permissions Associate (Pictures)
Robyn Young, Imaging and Multimedia Content Editor
Pamela A. Reed, Imaging Coordinator

Rita Wimberley, Senior Buyer
Evi Seoud, Assistant Manager, Composition Purchasing and Electronic Prepress

Kenn Zorn, Senior Art Director
Pamela A. E. Galbreath, Senior Art Designer

Linda Mahoney, LM Design, Typesetting

Cover photographs: Reproduced by permission of the Library of Congress.

Library of Congress Cataloging-in-Publication Data
Pendergast, Tom.
  Constitutional amendments from freedom of speech to flag burning / Tom Pendergast,
Sara Pendergast, and John Sousanis ; Elizabeth Shaw Grunow, editor.
    p. cm.
  Includes bibliographical references and index.
  ISBN 0-7876-4865-5 (set: hardcover)-ISBN 0-7876-4866-3 (v.1)-ISBN 0-7876-4867-1
(v.2)-ISBN 0-7876-4868-X (v.3)
    1.Constitutional amendments-United States-Juvenile literature. 2. Constitutional
law-United States-Juvenile literature. 3. Civil rights-United States-Juvenile literature.
[1. Constitutional amendments. 2. Constitutional law. 3. Civil rights.] I. Title:
Constitutional amendments. II. Pendergast, Sara. III. Sousanis, John. IV. Title.

  KF4557 .P46 2001
  342.73'03-dc21

                                                                        00-067236

Printed in the United States of America

10 9 8 7 6 5 4 3 2 1

Contents

Volume 1

Contents

Contents

Reader's Guide

The Constitution of the United States has been the supreme law of the land for more than two centuries, since it was formally adopted in 1788. The Constitution's longevity as the basis for the U.S. government owes much to its original framers. Their decision to provide a system of checks and balances among the various branches of government and to create a form of representation that took into account the interests of big and small states left room for a growing country to adapt and reinterpret the Constitution. However, the Constitution has never been a purely static document: because the framers created a process for amending the Constitution, over the years the document has been changed and expanded in response to changes in American society. It is a process that is never taken lightly, for it means tinkering with the very framework of the nation's political system. Yet from the years immediately following its ratification through the 1990s, Americans have successfully amended the Constitution twenty-seven times, and made attempts to change it numerous other times.

Constitutional Amendments: From Freedom of Speech to Flag Burning devotes a single chapter to each of the existing amendments to the United States Constitution as well as a final chapter that looks at several amendment proposals that have not been ratified.

An Introduction provides general information about the drafting of the Constitution, the interpretive powers of the Supreme Court, and the ratification process that supplements the information provided for each of the individual amendments.

Chapters average approximately six thousand words in length and examine the historical origins of the amendment, the drafting and ratifi-

cation of the amendment, and the consequent impact the amendment has had on American society. In general, cases pertaining to an amendment are discussed in chronological order. However, in some instances an amendment's various clauses are discussed separately in order to clarify the particular significance of each clause.

Additional Features

Constitutional Amendments is organized for easy fact-finding:

- Each chapter is headed by the full text of the constitutional amendment it is covering.

- Standard sidebars containing the ratification facts of each amendment also appear at the beginning of each chapter.

- The issues and amendments are presented in language accessible to middle school users.

- Challenging terms are sometimes used, so a Words to Know section is included in each volume. The section defines words and terms used in the set that may be unfamiliar to students.

- Sources for further study are included at the end of each chapter.

- The three volumes also contain more than 150 photos and illustrations to further enhance the text.

- Each of the three volumes also includes a research topics section and a general subject index for locating key people, places, events, and cases discussed throughout *Constitutional Amendments*.

Suggestions Are Welcome

We welcome your comments on *Constitutional Amendments: From Freedom of Speech to Flag Burning*. Please write, Editors, *Constitutional Amendments,* U•X•L, 27500 Drake Road, Farmington Hills, MI 48331-3535; call toll-free: 1-800-877-4253; fax to 248-414-5043; or send e-mail via http://www.galegroup.com.

Advisory Board

Special thanks are due for the invaluable comments and suggestions provided by U•X•L's *Constitutional Amendments advisors:*

- Connie Altimore, American History teacher, Northeast Middle School, Midland, Michigan
- Nancy Guidry, Young Adult Librarian, Santa Monica Public Library, Santa Monica, California
- Ann Marie LaPrise, Children's Librarian and Assistant Manager, Elmwood Park Branch, Detroit Public Library, Detroit, Michigan

Contributors

The following writers contributed to U•X•L's *Constitutional Amendments:*

- John Sousanis, chapters 1-10, 12
- Tina Gianoulis, chapters 11, 16, 24, 27
- Richard Clay Hanes, chapters 13-15
- Sara Pendergast, chapters 17, 25
- Tom Pendergast, chapters 18, 21, 22, 23 (with Tim Seul), 28
- Tim Seul, chapters 19, 20, 23 (with Tom Pendergast), 26

Research and Activity Ideas

The following list of research and activity ideas is intended to offer suggestions for complementing social studies and history curricula, to trigger additional ideas for enhancing learning, and to suggest cross-disciplinary projects for library and classroom use.

Discussing a Free Press: The First Amendment limits government interference with a free press. Consider how the news media might differ if the government were allowed to directly influence or censor the press. Make a list of all the stories in a single edition of a newspaper or weekly news magazine. Have students discuss which stories might be censored if the First Amendment didn't exist. Physically cut these stories from the publication to demonstrate the impact the Amendment has had. For further discussion, have students suggest stories that a government-controlled press might add to a newspaper, such as articles praising officials or government actions. Finally, discuss the impact a government-controlled press might have on today's society.

Religious Diversity: The First Amendment's Establishment Clause helps protect religious diversity in the United States. Using almanacs, census data, or other sources, create graphs and charts that compare how many different religions are practiced in your community, your county, and your state. Discuss how life might be different if there were a single government-established religion.

Debating the Right to Bear Arms: Over the years the Second Amendment has been interpreted quite differently by different groups. Groups debate whether the amendment simply protects a

state's right to establish a militia or whether it also guarantees the individual's right to own weapons. After discussing the chapter on the Second Amendment divide the class in half, with each half taking one side of the debate. The students in each group should work together to rewrite the amendment in a way they believe clearly states their side of the debate. Then have the entire class discuss how the proposed amendments would affect today's society.

Living the Third Amendment: The Third Amendment limits the practice of quartering (or housing) soldiers in private homes. During the French and Indian War, American colonist were sometimes forced to house British soldiers in their homes. Imagine that your family has been asked to house one or more soldiers. Write a journal entry discussing how such an arrangement might impact your daily life.

Voting Rights: The Fifteenth, Nineteenth and Twenty-sixth Amendments granted the right to vote to groups of people who were previously denied the right. To help students understand the importance of political participation, divide the class into groups by gender, birth months, or other criteria. Then put several fictitious decisions up for a vote, such as which popular band the class would like to invite to play at the school or which team sport should be cut from the school's athletic program. With each vote, look at how the results would differ if one or another group's votes were not counted. Discuss the impact of limiting or widening the number of people allowed to vote in real elections.

Government Bans: Look at the history of the temperance (anti-alcohol) movement. Discuss why the Eighteenth Amendment prohibition on alcohol sales and consumption was passed and the reasons the Twenty-first Amendment later repealed it. Consider the difficulties of establishing a complete ban on other products considered unhealthy or dangerous, such as cigarettes.

Interpreting Amendments: Over the years the Supreme Court has changed the way it interprets various Constitutional amendments. Track the Court's changing interpretation of a particular amendment from the time it was passed to the present day. Discuss how the same amendment could be understood differently at different times in history and by different justices.

Draft a New Amendment: Divide your class into groups and have each group choose an issue they feel strongly about. Have the group write a proposal for a constitutional amendment that incorporates their idea. Issues could range from serious political issues to more frivolous ideas such as imposing a national dress code. Each group should then present its amendment for debate with the rest of the class. Discuss whether the amendments might be interpreted to mean something other than what the drafters intended. After the class discussion, allow each group to rewrite their amendment. Finally, put the redrafted amendments up for a vote of the class.

Unratified Amendments: Chapter twenty-eight looks at a number of unratified constitutional amendments. Have students write an essay on how American society might be different if one of these amendments were ratified.

Research and Activity Ideas

Words to Know

A

Abolition: Total opposition to all slavery.

Abolitionists: Those who fought for an end to slavery.

Abortion: A biological event or medical procedure that terminates a pregnancy.

Abridge: To lessen.

Absentee ballot: A ballot that can be mailed in, so that a person can vote if they are away from home during an election.

Abstinence: The act of abstaining or avoiding something, for instance, the use of alcoholic beverages.

Acquittal: A trial outcome in which a defendant is free from a charge.

Activist: Someone who works hard for a political cause.

Aerial surveillance: Watching activity from the air, usually in a helicopter or airplane.

Affirmation: A solemn declaration.

Appeal: A legal proceeding in which a case is taken before a higher court for rehearing.

Apportionment: The process of determining how many representatives a particular state, county, or other kind of region should send to a legislature.

Words to Know

Articles of Confederation: An early constitution for the United States that set up a weak central government. The document was ratified in 1781 but was replaced by the U.S. Constitution in 1789.

Assistance of counsel: The help of outsiders in a trial. The term usually applies to the aid of a professional attorney.

Attorney: A person who is legally qualified to represent someone or some group in a court of law. A lawyer.

B

Billet: Lodging for troops in nonmilitary buildings.

Bill of Rights: The first ten amendments to the U.S. Constitution. These amendments clarify certain personal freedoms not clearly defined in the language of the Constitution.

Bipartisan: Supported by two groups/political parties.

Bond: A certificate issued by a company or government that promises to pay back the cost of the certificate with interest.

Bootlegging: The illegal manufacture, sale, or transportation of liquor.

Bounty: A reward for performing a certain task.

Boycott: A political tactic by which a group of people refuse to use a product or service to protest something they don't like about the producers of the product or service.

British Empire: Worldwide territories governed by or linked to Great Britain.

C

Candidate: A person nominated for a political office.

Capital crime: A crime that is punishable by death.

Capital gains: The profit that is made from selling something.

Civil rights: A series of basic rights written in the Constitution and identified through time that are to be enjoyed by all citizens without undue government interference.

Civil trial: A trial in which a person (or group) who has been injured seeks payment from the person who caused the injury. In a civil trial the person bringing the case to the court is seeking a remedy (solution) to a problem, whereas in a criminal trial an entity (usually the state) is seeking to have someone punished for an illegal action.

Civil War: War fought between the Northern (Union) states and the Southern (Confederate) states from 1861 to1865 over issues such as state and federal power and the future of slavery in the United States.

Coalition: A temporary alliance of different groups seeking a similar goal.

Cold War: A state of political tension between the Soviet Union and the United States that lasted from roughly 1947 to 1989.

Colony: A territory controlled by a distant government.

Commerce: The large-scale exchange of goods and products involving transportation.

Common law: Legal tradition. Many of America's legal traditions can be traced to English common law.

Compensation: Something given to someone in return for something else; often, payment given in exchange for work performed.

Compromise of 1850: A political deal aimed at easing the conflict between slave and free states, this compromise allowed California to join the United States as a free state in exchange for giving slave owners the right to travel into free territory to capture runaway slaves.

Compulsory process: A process by which courts subpoena (command someone to appear in court) witnesses for the defense and prosecution.

Confederacy: Also known as the Confederate States of America; the eleven Southern states that seceded, or withdrew, from the United States during the Civil War (1861–65).

Congress: The legislative, or law making, branch of the U.S. government. Congress is made up of two parts, called houses: the Senate and the House of Representatives. The Senate gives each state equal representation, while representation in the House of Representatives is roughly proportionate to the state's share of the country's total population.

Words to Know

Words to Know

Conscription: Compulsory enrollment in the armed forces; the draft.

Consensus: Widespread agreement; an opinion reached by the majority.

Construe: To interpret.

Consumer: Someone who uses or buys a product or service.

Conviction: A trial outcome in which a defendant is found guilty of a charge.

Corruption: Wrong-doing in government.

Criminal trial: A trial in which the government seeks to punish someone for a crime. In a criminal trial an entity (usually the state) is seeking to have someone punished for an illegal action, whereas in a civil trial the person bringing the case to the court is seeking a remedy (solution) to a problem.

D

Declaration of Independence: Completed on July 4, 1776, the document—which was written primarily by Thomas Jefferson—lists the complaints of the thirteen American colonies against Great Britain and formally announces their independence from the British Empire.

Deduction: In taxes, an expense a taxpayer can subtract from his/her taxable income.

Desecration: The violation of something sacred.

Discrimination: Giving privileges to one group but not to another similar group.

Diplomat: Someone who represents the government of his or her country during relations with other countries.

Direct election: An election in which people vote, not an election in which representatives vote in the place of the public.

Domestic product: Something that is made within a country. The opposite of domestic is foreign.

Due process: Proceedings carried out within established guidelines that do not limit or violate a person's legal rights.

E

Effective counsel: Helpful legal assistance.

Electors: Representatives from each state who cast the actual votes for president and vice president of the United States.

Electoral College: A body of electors, or representatives, from each state, who elect the president and vice president of the United States. These electors vote based on numbers gathered through the count of the popular vote in each state, which is the actual vote of the citizens of that state.

Electoral majority: Votes from a majority of the electors in the Electoral College.

Emancipation: The act of freeing one person from the control and authority of another.

Embargo: A government order forbidding trade with another country.

Eminent domain: Literally, the term means "highest claim to ownership of land." The concept allows a government to take private property for public use because the government is thought to have eminent domain over all the lands it rules.

Enumerated rights: Rights that are specifically defined in the Constitution or its amendments.

Enumeration: An official count, as of the number of citizens in a legislative district.

E pluribus unum: A Latin phrase meaning "Out of many, one." It is one of the mottoes of the United States.

Equal protection of the laws: A right that states that no person or class of persons can be denied the same protection of the laws pertaining to their lives, property, and pursuit of happiness as others in similar circumstances.

Equitable claim: A civil claim in which the plaintiff (person bringing suit in court) seeks to cause the defendant to perform certain actions (or to stop performing others). Equitable claims are not covered by the Seventh Amendment.

Ethics: Moral values.

Words to Know

Evangelical: Characterized by ardent or crusading enthusiasm. Evangelical churches actively seek to spread their message and recruit new members.

Exclusionary rule: A legal concept asserting that evidence found during an illegal search should not be used against a defendant in court. The exclusionary rule is a relatively recent concept in legal history that is now applied in most American criminal trials.

Excise tax: An extra charge added to the price of some domestic products.

Exemption: In taxes, part of the income on which the taxpayer is allowed not to pay taxes.

Express powers: Federal powers that are specifically enumerated or listed in the Constitution or its amendments.

F

Faithless elector: A term used to describe a representative who does not vote the way he or she had promised to before being selected to the Electoral College. By the end of the twentieth century, only eight electors in the history of the Electoral College had cast such "faithless" votes.

Farmer's alliances: Groups of farmers who met to discuss their problems and agree on common goals so that they could increase their political power and improve the conditions of their lives.

Federalism: The type of government in which separate states come together to form a union. Also, the kind of politics within such a government by which people believe the states should have their own identity and power separate from the national government.

Federalist Party: A political party founded in 1787 that argued for the establishment of a strong federal (central or national) government.

Federation: A government in which separate states unite for greater strength.

Filibuster: An attempt to obstruct the passage of legislation, often with prolonged speechmaking.

Flat tax: A tax with one rate for everyone.

Flogging: Very hard beating, usually with a whip or a stick.

Frisk: To search a person by running ones hand over the person's clothes and through his or her pockets.

Fruit from the poisonous tree: A term for evidence that is obtained as a direct result of other illegally obtained evidence. Such "fruit" is often not allowed to be used in court.

G

General warrant: A type of warrant (a document issued by a judge allowing the holder to search the premises) used by British officials until the end of the eighteenth century. A general warrant lacked probable cause and usually did not name specific people or places to be searched.

Good faith exception: A concept that allows illegally gained evidence to be used in court, if the police officer did not willfully break the law in obtaining it. Allows for honest mistakes by law enforcement officials.

Graduated tax: A tax where the rate increases in steps, little by little.

Grand jury: A group of citizens assembled to decide if the government has enough evidence against an accused person to justify holding a trial.

Great Britain: At the time of the American Revolution, Great Britain was a single state made up of England, Wales, and Scotland. Today, Great Britain, or the United Kingdom, also includes Northern Ireland. Great Britain ruled the thirteen American colonies until the American Revolution in 1776.

Great Depression: A worldwide economic collapse that began with the stock market crash of 1929.

Grievance: A complaint about an unjust act.

H

Historical test: The method used to determine which civil cases are entitled to a jury trial under the Seventh Amendment. If a case in federal courts historically would have been entitled to a jury trial under English common law, a jury is used.

Words to Know

House of Representatives: The lower house in Congress. Each state's representation in the house is roughly proportionate to its share of the total population. Every state has at least one representative.

I

Immunity: Exemption (to be excused) from regular legal requirements and penalties.

Impeachment: The process by which an elected official is removed from office.

Implied powers: Federal powers that are only hinted at or suggested by the Constitution.

Inauguration: The ceremony by which newly elected presidents and vice presidents are sworn into office.

Income: Money earned from working, investing, renting, or selling things.

Incriminate: To accuse or blame someone for a crime.

Indictment: A formal charge prepared by the government against a defendant that is agreed to by a grand jury or by a judge in a hearing.

Informant: A person who gives information or tips to law enforcement officers.

Insurrection: Rising up against established authority.

Integration: To bring together or blend; commonly used to describe a mixture of different races of people.

Internal Revenue Code (U.S. Tax Code): The collection of all the laws and rules that concern federal income tax.

Intervene: To come between.

Involuntary servitude: The state in which a person works for another person against his or her will due to force, imprisonment, or coercion, regardless of whether the person is being paid for their labor.

J

Jeopardy: Exposure to danger of death, loss, or injury. The type of danger a defendant is in while on trial for a criminal offense.

Jim Crow: Legally enforced racial segregation, named after a stereotypical black character in a minstrel show.

Jurisdiction: The power and authority to interpret and apply the law. A court has jurisdiction in a district, or defined area.

Just compensation: A fair payment for losses.

L

Lame duck: A name given to an elected official continuing in office during the period between a failed election bid and the inauguration of a successor. "Lame duck" politicians are thought to be ineffective and without power.

Legislature: An official law-making governmental body or assembly.

Literacy test: A test a voter had to pass before being able to vote in an election. The tests were considered controversial because they prevented those who were denied equal access to an education the right to vote.

Lynch: To execute someone without due process of law, often by hanging.

M

Magistrate: A judge or other court official capable of issuing a warrant.

Magna Carta: A document, signed by King John I of England in 1215, outlining personal and political freedoms granted to English citizens.

Majority: More than half of a total.

Mandate: A show of support by voters for their elected representative. A president is thought to have a mandate to enact his proposals when he receives broad popular support.

Maritime: Relating to navigation or commerce on the seas.

Miranda warnings: Standard warnings about rights and responsibilities that are read or spoken to a suspect in police custody before he or she is interrogated. The Supreme Court established the warnings in the case of *Miranda v. Arizona* (1966).

Missouri Compromise: A political deal aimed at easing the conflict between slave and free states, this 1820 compromise drew a line

across lands acquired in the Louisiana Purchase and declared that states admitted south of the line could allow slave holding but that states north of the line must be free.

Muckraking: Journalism that exposes corruption in public life.

N

Narrow interpretation: To greatly limit the meaning of something.

Naturalization: A process in which a person may gain citizenship by meeting certain requirements such as length of residence or act of Congress.

Nationalism: Within a federation, it is the political belief that the national government should be more powerful than the state governments.

Negotiate: To settle disagreements or resolve issues by discussion and mutual agreement.

Nominate: To appoint or propose a candidate for office.

P

Pacifist: Someone who believes that war or violence is the wrong way to settle disputes.

Parliament: Great Britain's legislative (law-making) assembly.

Particularity requirement: One of the conditions a warrant must meet to be deemed legal under the Fourth Amendment. To meet the particularity requirement, the warrant must list the particular people and places to be searched and the specific kinds of evidence that an officer hopes to obtain.

Party: Group of people organized with the purpose of directing government policies.

Patent: An official government grant giving someone the right to be the only one to make a product or perform a process that he or she invented for a certain period of time.

Patent law: Laws dealing with the ownership of new inventions and commercial processes.

Pensions: Regular payments of money other than for salary, such as for retirement or disability.

Peonage: Forcing a person against his or her will to work for another to pay a debt.

Per diem: Latin, meaning "per day;" the rate of payment a person receives per day.

Plaintiff: The party who sues in a civil action; a complainant; the prosecution—that is, a state or the United States representing the people—in a criminal case.

Plain view rule: A rule that allows officers to seize evidence they do not have a warrant for if they come across the evidence legally.

Plurality: In an election among three or more candidates, a number of votes cast for one candidate that is greater than the number cast for any other candidate, but that is still less than half of the total number of votes.

Plutocrat: A wealthy person with the power to influence government. A plutocracy is a government ruled by a wealthy class.

Police power: A recognized general legal authority not specifically mentioned in the U.S. Constitution that states hold to govern their citizens, lands, or natural resources.

Political appointment: A job within the government that is filled by a person chosen by an elected official.

Poll: A survey by which a random group of people are asked their opinions in order to predict how most people feel about a subject. The Gallup Poll is a respected and famous polling company.

Poll taxes: Fees charged to citizens to vote at the voting (polling) place.

Popular majority: More than half of the votes case by the voting public.

Popular vote: In the U.S. presidential election process, the votes cast by the public rather than by the Electoral College.

Precedent: An instance that serves as an example for dealing with similar situations.

President: The highest elected office in U.S. government. The leader of the executive branch of government.

Words to Know

Presidential disability: The inability of the President to function in office.

President Pro Tempore: Senator who presides over the Senate in the absence of the vice president. Also considered the Senate's presiding officer, the president pro tempore is included in the line of succession should the offices of the president and vice president become vacant.

Probable cause: Information that would lead a reasonable person to believe that an officer's request for a warrant is merited.

Procedural due process: The constitutional guarantee that one's liberty and property rights may not be affected unless reasonable notice and an opportunity to be heard in order to present a claim or defense are provided.

Progressive era: A period from roughly 1900 to 1920 during which many Americans supported the improvement of society through changes in government and social policy.

Progressive tax: A tax that is based upon a person's ability to pay; the more a person earns or has, the more he or she pays in tax.

Prohibition: A period from 1920 to 1933 when the Eighteenth Amendment to the Constitution made the manufacture, sale, or transportation of intoxicating liquors within the United States illegal.

Prosecute: To begin civil or criminal legal proceedings.

Prosecutor: The government attorney in a criminal case.

Public rights: Rights created by Congress that were not in existence at the time the Bill of Rights was adopted. These rights are not subject to the traditions of common law.

R

Radical: Extreme. A radical change is a complete change; a person who is a radical advocates complete change of a system.

Ratification: A process in which three-fourths of the states must approve proposed amendments to the Constitution before the amendment can become formally adopted.

Reasonable expectation of privacy: One of the standards used to determine if a warrant is required to gather evidence. If a person has good reason to expect privacy (such as in their home or their car) a warrant is usually required before searching is permitted.

Redcoat: Slang term for British soldiers that refers to their bright red uniform jackets.

Regressive tax: A tax by which everyone is charged the same rate of tax, no matter how much property or income they may have.

Repeal: To revoke or rescind an official act or law. In the United States the repeal movement was directed to revoking the Eighteenth Amendment; it succeeded in 1933 with the passage of the Twenty-first Amendment.

Republic: A form of government in which government officials are elected by voters.

Retroactive: Something that applies to time already past.

Revenue: The income of a government.

S

Scandal: An embarrassing or dishonest action that offends the public and damages someone's reputation.

Secede: To break away from an organization.

Second Great Awakening: A period between roughly 1820 and 1850 when religious enthusiasm swept the country and church attendance grew dramatically.

Segregation: Keeping racial groups from mixing, such as maintaining separate facilities for members of different races or restricting use of facilities to members of one race.

Seizure: The forcible taking of property or other evidence.

Senate: The upper house of Congress. Two senators represent each state equally in the Senate.

Servitude: Owning another person who performs duties.

Union: Name given to the states that did not secede, or withdraw, from the United States during the Civil War (1861–65). The term also refers to a group of workers who unite in order to bargain (set wages and working conditions) with their employer.

Unit rule: A rule that gives all of a state's electoral votes to representatives of the party that wins the popular vote in that state.

V

Valid: Having legal authority or force.

Verdict: The formal decision or finding made by a jury concerning the questions submitted to it during a trial. The jury reports the verdict to the court, which generally accepts it.

Vice president: The second highest elected office in U.S. government. The vice president serves as the president of the Senate and also serves as president if the president is unable to do so.

W

Waive: To willingly give up a right, title, or something that is rightfully due to you.

Warrant: A document issued by a judge allowing the holder to search the premises.

Whig Party: A political party of the nineteenth century that was formed to oppose the Democratic Party. The Whigs encouraged the loose interpretation of the Constitution.

Wiretap: Any electronic device that allows eavesdropping on phone conversations.

Writs of assistance: A form of warrant once used by British officials in the American colonies. The general warrant allowed nearly unlimited searches and seizures of property.

Wrong-winner argument: An argument that states that, under certain circumstances, the Electoral College system in the United States could elect a president that was not, in fact, the people's choice.

Introduction: The Constitution and the Amendment Process

The United States Constitution and its twenty-seven amendments comprise the supreme law of the United States of America. Together they create the structure of American government: granting powers to the branches of government while simultaneously imposing strict limits on those powers. Although written more than two centuries ago, the Constitution has proven able to adapt to the changes in American society—while also helping to shape many of those changes. The ratified constitutional amendments altered aspects of the way Americans govern themselves, and most have had a lasting legal and cultural impact.

A New Nation is Born

In the years before the American Revolutionary War (1775–83) the thirteen original states were individual colonies governed by the British government. The men and women who lived in these territories tended to identify themselves as citizens of the individual colonies (such as Virginians or New Yorkers) rather than as part of a larger America.

In the early 1700s, the colonists found themselves increasingly at odds with the British government over issues such as taxation, tariffs, and the increased presence of the British Army in the colonies (see chapter three). There was a growing feeling within the colonies that Great Britain was infringing upon individual liberties (freedoms). Citizens of the various colonies began to band together in opposition to British rule.

Introduction

As political tension grew within the colonies, military tension grew between the colonial militias (bands of citizen soldiers) and British troops. The first battle of the American Revolution broke out in the spring of 1775. On July 4, 1776, the colonies signed the Declaration of Independence, formally calling for an end to the colonies' political connection to Great Britain. After six years of fighting, the colonies' Continental Army won the last battle of the American Revolutionary War in 1781. The superior leadership of General George Washington (1732–1799) led the colonies to their independence. He eventually became the first president of the United States.

Surprisingly enough, after their successful military cooperation, the thirteen states found that they now valued their independence not only from Great Britain, but also from one another.

The Articles of Confederation: A "league of friendship"

Not surprisingly, when the newly liberated states agreed to form a central government under a document known as the Articles of Confederation and Perpetual Union (commonly referred to as the Articles of Confederation), the government they set up had very little power of its own.

The Articles had originally been drafted in 1776, but were revised and approved by representatives of the thirteen colonies in November 1777. The original proposal was supposed to have created a powerful central government, but by the time the articles were ratified (agreed to) by several states in 1781, the document had been changed dramatically.

Under the Articles of Confederation, the federal (central or national) government was "a firm league of friendship" between the states. The Continental Congress, set up by the Articles of Confederation, was made up of a single assembly (or house) in which each state had only one vote. Nine of the thirteen votes were needed to pass any significant laws, and a unanimous vote was required to change the Articles. There also was no president under the Articles of Confederation, and the national courts were given legal power over very few cases.

SHAYS' REBELLION. The government under the Articles of Confederation was too weak to levy and collect taxes and could neither pay the country's debts nor defend the nation's borders. But it was a military uprising led by Massachusetts farmers that called many politicians' attention to the government's limitations. A severe depression (economic downturn) in the 1780s caused hundreds of farmers to lose their homes and land to debt. In what became known as Shays' Rebellion, several hundred farmers in Massachusetts banded together to protest the farmers' plights. Led by Daniel Shays, a former captain in the Continental Army, the farmers took over courthouses in five counties in the summer and fall of 1786.

Then in January 1787, the farmers marched on federal troops in Springfield, Massachusetts. After ten days of fighting, the federal troops put down the rebellion. But the battle convinced many political leaders that America's central government had to be strengthened. Shortly after Shays' Rebellion, the Continental Congress invited delegates from the states to a convention in Philadelphia, Pennsylvania, to revise the Articles of Confederation.

The Philadelphia Convention: Crafting a Stronger Government

The Philadelphia Convention began in May 1787. Interestingly, although the conventioneers were supposed to be working out a plan for strengthening the national government, the convention ended up being divided between Federalists, who favored a stronger central government, and Anti-Federalists, who opposed giving the central government any more power than it already had.

Several prominent Federalists such as James Madison (1751–1836) and Virginia governor Edmund Randolph (1753–1813) were among the first delegates to arrive in Philadelphia. They quickly drafted the so-called "Virginia Plan," which proposed scrapping the Articles of Confederation altogether to create a strong central government consisting of "supreme Legislative, Executive, and Judiciary" branches. The first delegates to attend the convention quickly adopted the Virginia Plan.

As more delegates arrived at the convention, however, the number of Anti-Federalists in attendance grew. The Anti-Federalists believed that the Articles of Confederation needed only a few amendments to make the existing government as effective as it needed to be. The Anti-Federalists plan, known as the "New Jersey Plan," called for giving the central government far less power than the Virginia Plan did.

As each article of the already adopted Virginia Plan was debated at the convention, the Anti-Federalists chipped away at the plan, until the two sides arrived at system of government that represented a compromise between the Federalists and the Anti-Federalists.

The Constitution of the United States.

Reproduced by permission of

Archive Photos, Inc.

The Constitution of the United States: A Delicate Balancing Act

Although the new Constitution called for a strong central government, the states also retained a great deal of power. This system of "dual sovereignty" (two powers) allowed both governments to exist at once.

The Constitution created at the Philadelphia convention gave the central government specific powers. The states, on the other hand, were to retain any government powers they already had had that were not specifically granted to the central government. This division of power between the central government and the state governments, known as the federal system of government, remains in place to this day.

The central government under the Constitution is divided into three branches: legislative, executive, and judicial. The legislative (lawmaking) branch of government is the Congress. The executive branch is led by the President, and is responsible for enforcing federal laws and carrying out national policies. The judicial branch, the national court system headed by the Supreme Court, is responsible for cases arising from federal and constitutional laws.

Each branch of government is granted specific areas of responsibility, but the Constitution also gives each branch some oversight of the others. This system of "checks and balances" between the branches of government is intended to prevent any branch from becoming too powerful.

Congress: The two-house compromise

The self-interests of the various states at the convention led to the formation of a unique legislative body. Large states argued that the number of representatives each state sent to the legislature (Congress) should be based on the states' population (how many people lived in each state). Southern states, which had large populations of slaves at the time, argued that they should be able to count the slaves when determining how many representatives they sent to Congress. Delegates from smaller states argued for equal representation for every state, regardless of its population. Delegates from the northern states, where slavery was far less common, however, opposed the use of slaves in determining representation.

The convention eventually reached a compromise, creating a Congress made up of two houses, or assemblies. In the upper house of Congress—the Senate—each state would be represented by two senators, giving the states equal standing. However, in the lower house of Congress—the House of Representatives—a state's representation would be determined by the relative size of its population (the larger a state's population, the more representatives that state sent to the House of Representatives). Bills (proposed laws) must be passed by both houses before they could become law.

Additionally, the Convention agreed that a state's population would be determined by counting the number of free persons (non-slaves) in the state and adding "three-fifths of all other Persons" [slaves] while "excluding Indians," who neither voted nor were taxed. (Slavery was abolished altogether in 1865 by the Thirteenth Amendment [see chapter thirteen]).

Article I, section 8 of the Constitution outlines most of the powers granted to Congress. These include the power to impose taxes, to provide for the common defense and general welfare of the United States, and to regulate commerce. Congress was also empowered to create a national currency (money), a postal system, and a system of courts below the Supreme Court. Only Congress can declare war and is given the power to raise and support an army and navy. More generally, the Constitution's "necessary and proper" clause states that Congress has the power "to make all laws which shall be necessary and proper for carrying into execution the foregoing powers, and all other powers vested by the Constitution in the government of the United States."

The president oversees many different aspects of running the country. Reproduced by permission of AP/Wide World Photos.

The Executive Branch: All the president's men

Under Article II of the Constitution, the president holds executive (or administrative) power. Presidents are elected to a four-year term by an Electoral College, made up of electors chosen by each of the states (see chapter twelve).

The president is the commander-in-chief of the nation's armed forces, and is responsible for ensuring that federal laws are "faithfully executed," which gives the president control over federal law enforcement agencies. The president also is responsible for appointing judges and federal officials and has the power to negotiate treaties (agreements) with other nations.

The vice president serves as president of the Senate and casts the deciding vote in any tie votes in that house. The vice president has few other powers, but must step in for the president if the president is unable to perform the executive duties.

The Judicial Branch: Supreme powers

Article III of the Constitution establishes the Supreme Court as the highest court in the United States. Congress may also create any lower courts it deems necessary. Federal judges are appointed for life, so that they will be less likely to give in to political pressure when deciding cases.

Federal courts hear cases arising from federal laws, or cases in which the federal government is involved, or where citizens from two different states are involved. The Supreme Court, however, generally hears cases only on appeal, that is, when a party in the case requests that the Court reconsider the ruling of a lower court. The Supreme Court's decisions cannot be appealed, and the Court serves as the final interpreter

The Supreme Court in 1868. Reproduced by permission of the Corbis Corporation (Bellevue).

of the laws of the United States, including all matters dealing with the Constitution and its amendments.

The Court consisted of six justices (judges) until 1869, when it was officially expanded to nine justices. In deciding cases, justices may write individual opinions (written explanations of the justice's reasoning in a case) or sign another justice's opinion. Regardless of how many opinions the Court issues in a case, its final ruling is decided by a simple vote of the justices.

Because it is the final interpreter of law in the United States, the Supreme Court has played a significant role in the history of the Constitution's various amendments.

Checks and balances: The branches' overlapping powers

As stated above, each of the three branches of government exercises some oversight of the others. The Senate must approve all treaties negotiated by the executive branch. While the president is commander-in-chief of the armed forces, only Congress can declare war. The president, on the other hand, may veto (reject) any bill passed by Congress. Once vetoed, a two-thirds majority in both houses of Congress must pass a bill for it to become law.

While the president appoints all federal judges and government officers, the Senate must also approve those appointments. Furthermore, the House of Representatives has the power to impeach (officially accuse of legal misconduct) judges and government officials. Once impeached, these officials (including the president) may be tried in the Senate, and if convicted may be removed from office.

Finally, the Supreme Court may use its power to interpret laws and the Constitution to strike down any laws or government actions it deems illegal or unconstitutional.

Ratifying the Constitution: A Question of Rights

Despite the Constitution's federal system of state and central government, and the system of checks and balances, many delegates to the Constitutional Convention worried that the new government would become too powerful. Toward the end of the convention, a debate began over whether the Constitution should include a bill of rights (a specific list of the people's rights).

James Madison drafted the original amendments that would become the Bill of Rights. Courtesy of the Library of Congress.

Anti-Federalists argued that without a bill of rights, the central government might eventually take away individual rights. The Federalists, however, argued that there was no need to spell out individual rights since the new government could only exercise those powers expressed in the Constitution.

According to Article VII of the Constitution, a minimum of nine of the thirteen states had to ratify the document before it could go into effect. In the months that followed the convention, Anti-Federalists continued to raise the issue of a bill of rights with the public. Having just fought to get rid of the powerful British government, many citizens were afraid of giving the new government too much power without some sort of declaration of the people's rights.

Federalists initially argued against the inclusion of a bill of rights. But in order to win approval for the new constitution, they eventually promised that Congress would add a bill of rights to the Constitution during its first session.

The first amendments: Crafting the Bill of Rights

The Federalists kept their word. From the hundreds of proposals made by the states, James Madison, now a representative to the House, drafted seventeen amendment proposals, which he presented to Congress

Introduction

on June 8, 1789. Over the next three months, Congress revised Madison's suggestions into twelve amendment proposals, which were then passed to the states for ratification. While the states were considering the proposed amendments, Vermont became the fourteenth state on March 4, 1791. Under the rules set out in the Constitution, this meant that eleven states (three-fourths of the existing states) were needed to ratify the constitutional amendments.

Though two of the proposed amendments were rejected (one would later become the Twenty-seventh Amendment), on December 15, 1791, Virginia became the eleventh state to approve the ten amendments that became the Bill of Rights. These amendments set out specific limits to the exercise of government power while guaranteeing certain rights to citizens, especially in regard to court and police actions.

- The First Amendment prohibits Congress from passing any law that abridges (decreases) the existing freedom of speech, religion, or the press (the media).

- The Second Amendment guarantees the "people's right to keep and bear arms [weapons]."

- The Third Amendment limits the government's ability to quarter (or house) soldiers in private homes.

- The Fourth Amendment prohibits unreasonable search and seizure.

- The Fifth Amendment includes several protections for people accused of crimes, including protection against "double jeopardy" (being tried twice for the same crime) and the right not to testify against oneself in trial.

- The Sixth Amendment provides the right to a speedy trial by jury in criminal cases.

- The Seventh Amendment provides for jury trials in civil cases.

- The Eighth Amendment prohibits the setting of excessive bail and fines, and forbids cruel and unusual punishments.

- The Ninth Amendment states that the rights listed in the Constitution are not the only rights retained by the people.

- The Tenth Amendment states that any powers not specifically granted to the federal government are retained by the states and the people, unless the Constitution specifically prohibits the use of such powers.

The Changing Constitution: Proposing and Ratifying Constitutional Amendments

Those first additions and changes to the Constitution were made according to rules spelled out in the Constitution. In fact, Article V of the Constitution sets out two methods for amending the Constitution.

In the first method, Congress may propose an amendment with a two-thirds vote of both the Senate and the House of Representatives. If the proposal passes in both houses, the amendment must then be ratified by three-fourths of the states, either in state-wide conventions or by votes in the states' legislatures (law-making assemblies).

Under the second method, Congress can call for a constitutional convention for the proposal of new amendments. Congress can call for such a convention only if the legislatures from at least two-thirds of the states request that Congress do so.

Any proposals drafted at such a convention must then be ratified by three-fourths of the states. To date, however, the Constitution has only been amended through the first method.

Amending the Constitution is quite difficult. It requires an enormous degree of consensus (agreement) at the state and federal level. The

The Constitution and the Amendment Process

Abraham Lincoln worked to ensure the emancipation of slaves from their owners. Courtesy of the Library of Congress.

framers of the Constitution wanted to make sure that changes to the government were not made lightly. Indeed, in the two hundred-plus years since the Bill of Rights was ratified, only seventeen other amendments have been adopted by the states.

- The Eleventh Amendment (1798) prohibits the Supreme Court from hearing any lawsuits brought against one state by a citizen of another state.

- The Twelfth Amendment (1804) changed the way the president and vice president are elected. The amendment was drafted in response to the election of 1800. At the time, the offices of president and vice president were voted on separately. The party candidate who received the most votes would be president, and the candidate with the next highest number of votes would be vice president. In the election of 1800, one political party's presidential and vice presidential candidates accidentally received the same number of electoral votes for president, causing a great deal of confusion over who would serve as president.

- The Thirteenth (1865), Fourteenth (1868) and Fifteenth (1870) Amendments— which abolished slavery, required states to enforce their laws fairly, and extended the vote to black males—were all passed in the wake of America's bloody Civil War (1860–64) between the Northern and Southern states.

- The Sixteenth Amendment (1913) overrode a technicality in the Constitution, and made it legal for the federal government to implement an income tax.

- The Seventeenth Amendment (1913) provides for the direct election of senators by voters in each state. The Constitution originally gave state legislatures the power to appoint a state's senators.

- The Eighteenth (1919) and Twenty-first Amendments (1933) reflected America's changing attitudes toward alcoholic beverages. The Eighteenth Amendment outlawed the sale and transportation of liquor in the United States, reflecting the nation's growing temperance (anti-alcohol) movement. By 1933, though, American attitudes toward the sale of alcohol had shifted again, and the Twenty-first Amendment repealed (reversed) the ban on liquor.

- The Nineteenth Amendment (1920) extended the vote to women, after nearly a century of vigorous campaigning for female suffrage (the right to vote).

OPPOSITE PAGE

The government works to make sure that everyone gets a fair chance to vote in elections. This is a Braille ballot for a blind voter.

Reproduced by permission of AP/Wide World Photos.

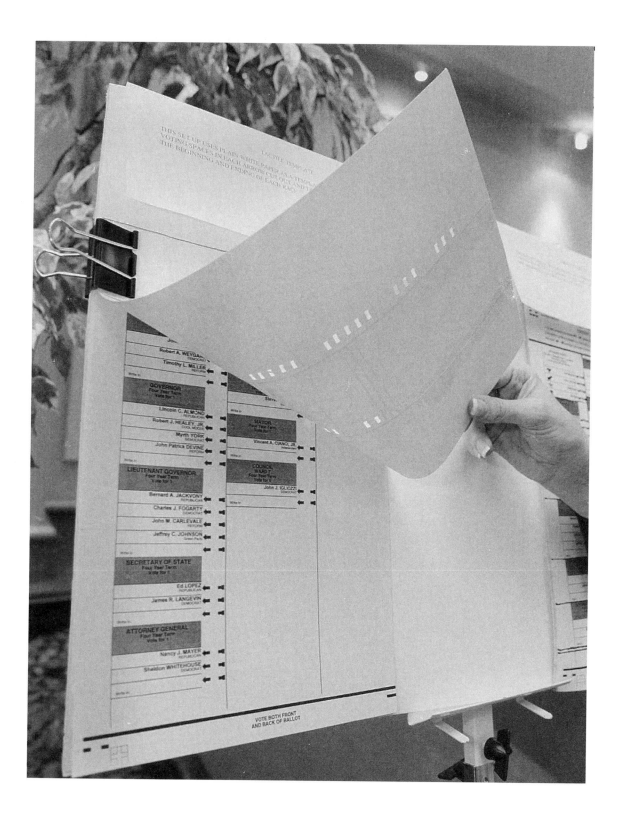

Introduction

- The Twentieth Amendment (1933) shortened the period between the time a person was elected to federal office and the time he or she took office.

- The Twenty-second Amendment (1951) prohibited any person from being elected to more than two terms as president, and was proposed after the death of Franklin D. Roosevelt, who was elected to four successive terms, beginning with the election of 1932.

- The Twenty-third Amendment (1961) gave residents of Washington D.C. (the nation's capital) the right to vote in presidential elections.

- The Twenty-fourth Amendment (1964) put an end to the practice of charging people a fee, or poll tax, to cast their vote in an election.

- The Twenty-fifth Amendment (1967) granted the president the power to nominate a new vice president whenever that office becomes vacant. The amendment also provides for the vice president to take over a president's duties when the president cannot perform those duties due to poor health or injury. This amendment was passed in the wake of the assassination of President John F. Kennedy in 1961. Vice President Lyndon B. Johnson assumed the presidency, leaving the vice president's office vacant for the remainder of the term.

- The Twenty-sixth Amendment (1971) lowered the legal voting age from twenty-one to eighteen in all elections.

- The Twenty-seventh Amendment (1992) was one of the original twelve amendments proposed for the Bill of Rights in 1789. However, the amendment, which prohibits any pay raise Congress votes for itself from taking effect until the following election, was not ratified until the 1990s, when the issue became a popular political issue.

Additionally, Congress has passed a number of proposals for amendments that failed to be ratified by the necessary three-fourths of the states (see chapter twenty-eight).

Certainly, the Constitution's enduring power is due in part to the fact that the framers provided a method of amending the document when necessary. What is remarkable in discussing the Constitutional amendments, however, is how very rarely the American people have found it necessary to do so.

Constitutional Amendments

Eighteenth Amendment

SECTION 1: After one year from the ratification of this article the manufacture, sale, or transportation of intoxicating liquors within, the importation thereof into, or the exportation thereof from the United States and all territory subject to the jurisdiction thereof for beverage purposes is hereby prohibited.

SECTION 2: The Congress and the several States shall have concurrent powers to enforce this article by appropriate legislation.

SECTION 3: This article shall be inoperative unless it shall have been ratified as an amendment to the Constitution by the legislatures of the several States, as provided in the Constitution, within seven years from the date of the submission hereof to the States by the Congress.

The Eighteenth Amendment was one of the most controversial amendments ever added to the U.S. Constitution. Created by temperance advocates who had fought for years to limit Americans' consumption of alcohol, the amendment outlawed the manufacture, sale, or transportation of alcoholic beverages anywhere within the United States. The amendment kicked off a period known as Prohibition, a thirteen-year span during which federal and state governments created numerous laws, hired many new law enforcement agents, and overloaded the court systems in an often futile effort at keeping Americans from consuming alcohol.

This "noble experiment," as it was called by President Herbert Hoover, turned out to be a dismal failure. Huge numbers of Americans found ways to make or purchase alcohol and law enforcement agencies were overwhelmed with the difficulty of enforcing unpopular laws. In 1933 the Eighteenth Amendment became the first amendment to be repealed. It was revoked by the Twenty–first Amendment. In the end, the rise and fall of the Eighteenth Amendment was a dramatic story that pitted those who wanted to dictate a national morality against those who

Eighteenth Amendment

wanted to guarantee personal liberty. It was also a real test of how well the Constitution responded to the demands of the people.

Alcohol and Temperance: Two American Traditions

From the very founding of the United States, Americans have had a love-hate relationship with alcoholic beverages. Alcoholic beverages—beer, wine, and so-called hard liquors (with higher alcohol content) were popular with the very first colonists to come to North America. In colonial days, workers often drank beer on the job and sometimes even drank at church. Brewing beer and distilling liquor were some of the most successful of early industries in the British colonies, and they brought much-needed tax

Cotton Mather was an early colonial anti-drunkeness advocate. Courtesy of the Library of Congress.

revenues to the colonies. Alehouses, taverns, and inns often served as the social focal point of small communities, providing gathering places where people could catch up on news and gossip while having a drink. Finally, up until the mid-eighteenth century people believed that consuming moderate amounts of alcohol was good for one's health. Alcohol was sometimes even given to sick children.

As much as early Americans enjoyed alcohol, most of them also believed that it should be enjoyed in moderation. Leading members of the Revolutionary generation (the generation of thinkers who led the American Revolution) believed that the members of a republic must guard the public virtue, and urged the American people to renounce a range of self-indulgent behaviors, including drunkenness, in order to ensure a better society. Beginning in the late eighteenth century, many people began to make a distinction between drinking beer and wine and drinking hard liquor, such as whiskey and rum. (Hard liquor has a higher alcohol content and thus leads more quickly to drunkenness.)

On February 27, 1777, the Continental Congress passed a resolution urging state legislatures "to pass laws putting an immediate stop to the practice of distilling grain (the process used to make hard liquor), by which the most extensive evils are likely to be derived, if not quickly prevented," according to Paul Sann in *The Lawless Decade.* Ten years later, in 1788, the *American Museum* magazine commended those who celebrated the adoption of the Constitution by drinking beer and hard cider

and instructed its reader to "despise SPIRITOUS LIQUORS, as *Anti–federal,* and to consider them as the companions of all those vices, that are calculated to dishonour and enslave our country." Such articles urged people to be temperate—to enjoy weak alcoholic beverages in moderation.

The Temperance Tradition

Although Americans continued to be rather heavy drinkers into the nineteenth century, the members of a growing temperance movement began to offer more determined criticisms of this American tradition. The temperance movement was greatly aided in the early years of the century by the growth of evangelical Christian groups involved in the Second Great Awakening (a period between roughly 1820 and 1850 when religious enthusiasm swept the country). Methodists, Baptists, and Mormons all encouraged sobriety and virtue, but temperance was also backed by major politicians. Every American president from James Madison (in office from 1809–1817) to Abraham Lincoln (1861–1865) endorsed a pledge that declared that "ardent spirit, as a drink, is not only needless, but hurtful; and that the entire disuse of it would tend to promote the health, the virtue, and the happiness of the community."

Temperance clubs began to form in the early 1800s. According to Eileen Lucas, author of *The Eighteenth and Twenty–first Amendments: Alcohol—Prohibition and Repeal,* "Individuals and small groups of people began to profess that they would consume no more distilled spirits." Such groups soon began to try to persuade others about the evils of strong drink. Some societies asked their members to sign a pledge of total abstinence by placing a "T" after their name; they were soon called "teetotalers," a term that today means someone who abstains from drinking any alcohol. In the 1820s and 1830s Connecticut preacher Lyman Beecher, father of writer Harriet Beecher Stowe, preached widely about the evils of drink, and attempted to form the first national temperance society.

The War Against Drink

By the mid-nineteenth century the temperance campaign had become much more serious. Temperance leaders soon changed their tactics; instead of trying to persuade drinkers to quit, they tried to pass laws barring the sale of alcohol. Maine politician Neal Dow was among the first to succeed at passing such laws. Transformed by his experience trying to rescue a rel-

ative from his drinking habit, Dow vowed to shut down the saloons in his state. In 1851 he pushed through a law in Maine called "An Act for the Suppression of Drinking Houses and Tippling Shops," the strongest prohibition law ever passed in the United States. Twelve other states followed suit, though several of these measures were ruled unconstitutional.

TEMPORARY SETBACK. The legal war against drink was temporarily stalled during and just after the Civil War, for the federal government discovered that the taxation of alcohol provided a reliable source of revenue. Lincoln's Internal Revenue Act of 1862 charged a fee to any establishment that

Temperance leaders such as Carry Nation attracted a lot of attention to the prohibition cause. Courtesy of the Library of Congress.

CARRY NATION

Carry Nation was among the most determined and colorful of the prohibition crusaders. She became famous for carrying a hatchet into saloons to attack bottles and kegs of offending alcohol, and lectured nationally on the evils of drink.

Born Carry Amelia Moore on November 25, 1846, Carry endured a difficult childhood. Her family moved frequently, and her mother suffered from delusions that she was Queen Victoria of England (she was later placed in a hospital for the insane). Carry was forced to work from an early age to support her poor family, but was often unable to work because of a series of vague illnesses. When she met and became engaged to a young doctor named Charles Gloyd she must have thought her troubles had come to an end, but she soon discovered that Gloyd was a hopeless drunk who spent most of his time drinking at a local fraternal lodge (Gloyd had hidden his drinking before their marriage in 1867). Carry and her infant daughter left Gloyd within a year to move back with her parents. Gloyd died of alcoholism six months later.

Carry's second marriage in 1877, to an older lawyer, minister, and editor named David Nation, was little happier. The couple argued constantly, and David was scornful of her religious extremism. By 1889 the Nations had moved to Medicine Lodge, Kansas, where Carry helped start a local chapter of the Women's Christian Temperance Union (WCTU) in 1892. Her extreme views and intolerance alienated many,

served alcohol and a tax on the manufacture of liquor or beer. Such taxes would remain an important source of income for the government until the early 1900s. Temperance advocates complained that the tax granted drinking establishments the respectability of government approval.

THE NATIONAL PROHIBITION PARTY AND THE WOMEN'S CHRISTIAN TEMPERANCE UNION. Temperance leaders reorganized themselves in 1869 into the National Prohibition Party. The party called for the vote for women and for the direct election of senators, two measures it thought would help ensure more support for temperance efforts (both measures would later

including her husband, who finally divorced her in 1901. By then, however, Carry had become wed to her anti–alcohol crusade.

Nation began her crusade in her home town of Medicine Lodge by marching into the local saloon and telling the bartender that he would go to hell unless he shut down. Within a few months he was out of business, and Nation exerted similar pressure on the town's other drinking establishments. In 1900, obeying what she called a command from the Lord, she traveled to the nearby town of Kiowa, strode into a saloon, and bellowed to the men drinking there, according to Carleton Beals in *Cyclone Carry,* "Men! I have come to save you from a drunkard's fate." She proceeded to smash every bottle she could find, and then to stand in the street challenging the mayor and the police to arrest her. They did not, though the police in other towns would not prove so lenient. Nation was later jailed for similar attacks, though her jailing did not stop her crusade. (However, the WCTU thought her attacks were too extreme and did not give her open support.)

Nation became ever more bold in her attacks in the first decade of the twentieth century. Carrying her trademark hatchet, she and her female followers would sing songs and pray in front of saloons before venturing inside to berate the drinkers and smash the drink. Nation published several newsletters, including *The Hatchet* and *The Smasher's Mail,* and in 1904 published her autobiography, *The Use and the Need of the Life of Carry A. Nation.* In declining health for years, Nation collapsed after giving a speech in Eureka Springs, Arkansas, in 1911. She spent the remaining months of her life in mental confusion and died on June 2, 1911.

become Constitutional amendments). The party also proposed, as part of its platform for the presidential election of 1872, that the Constitution be amended to establish prohibition—the complete ban on the manufacture and sale of alcohol. The platform and the presidential candidate, James Black, a Philadelphia lawyer, did not succeed, but they planted a seed that would grow until the passage of such an amendment fifty years later.

An even more powerful force in the ongoing battle against alcohol was the Women's Christian Temperance Union (WCTU). Founded in 1874, the WCTU became the largest women's organization of the late nineteenth century, with over 175,000 members. Promoting prohibition

as a benefit to the family, its members tried to influence local politicians to support their policies (which grew to include women's suffrage, or voting, and reforms in divorce laws, property rights, and education). But they also created a dramatic public presence by invading bars and saloons, singing and praying, and either blocking access to or actually smashing bottles of alcohol. WCTU member Carry Nation attracted national attention with her dramatic and violent attacks on saloons.

Members of groups like the National Prohibition Party, the WCTU, and the Anti-Saloon League argued for prohibition on similar grounds. Alcohol, they believed, posed real dangers to the social institutions—family, church, work—on which the nation was based. Alcohol stole men from their families, and encouraged men to skip work and frequent prostitutes. Saloons, said critics, were dens of sin, evil places that tempted men away from their responsibilities. America would be a better place, they reasoned, if people simply had no access to alcohol.

Prohibition and the Progressive Era

By the 1890s times were changing in America. Great numbers of immigrants were pouring into American cities, where huge factories and industries sprang up. Political bosses increasingly ran such cities, often by "buying" the votes of the newly-arrived immigrants. At the same time, new western states were being admitted to the Union. The citizens of these predominantly rural new states were critical of the excessive influence that large industries and industrial leaders exerted on American politics. These major social conflicts gave rise to what is known as the Progressive Era, a period from roughly 1900 to 1920 in which many Americans organized to reform political and social institutions. During this time middle-class, Protestant Americans joined together to promote their social agenda—an important part of which was prohibition.

Kansas became the first state to make prohibition part of its state constitution in 1881; other states followed. By 1918 there were twenty–six states with some laws regulating the liquor trade. In many cases, these laws were passed by middle-class, Protestant majorities who didn't like the lawlessness of the cities or the influence of immigrants, many of whom were Catholic and came from countries where drinking was a popular activity. In 1913 prohibitionists secured the passage of the Webb-Kenyon Bill, a federal law that gave dry, or non-drinking, states the right to stop liquor shipments at their borders. The Supreme Court ruled that the law was constitutional, giving cheer to the prohibitionists, who felt that the time was right to make prohibition the law of the land.

Victory!

By 1919 prohibitionists felt that the time had come to pass a constitutional amendment. The entrance of the United States into World War I gave them added fuel for their arguments: they claimed that grain was needed to support the war effort, not for making beer and liquor, and they stirred up hostility against American beer brewers, most of whom were of German ancestry. At the same time, Congress was growing increasingly friendly toward passing an amendment. From 1913 to 1919 the U.S. Congress had considered thirty–nine proposed amendments abolishing the liquor trade in the United States. But now, with the country at war, senators who had once resisted were willing to go along, on one condition. They insisted that the amendment had to be ratified by the states within seven years. Anti-prohibition forces felt that the prohibitionists could not convince enough states to pass the amendment within this time frame, and felt sure that the amendment would fail. They were wrong.

The Eighteenth Amendment was put before the Senate for a vote on August 1, 1917, and passed easily by a margin of sixty–five to twenty. On December 18, 1917, the amendment passed in the House of Representative by a margin of 282 to 128. Mississippi became the first state to

Those in favor of prohibition would often publish pamphlets and hang posters in an attempt to get their message across. This poster was entitled the "Women's Holy War." Courtesy of the Library of Congress.

Eighteenth Amendment

ratify the amendment on January 8, 1918. To the surprise of the wets (those opposed to Prohibition), it took just over a year for thirty–five more states to ratify the amendment. On January 16, 1919, Nebraska became the thirty–sixth state, thus ensuring that the Eighteenth Amendment would go into effect.

WIDESPREAD SUPPORT. Critics of Prohibition had claimed that Americans would never support such a determined suspension of their individual rights, but the support for the amendment among state lawmakers was far more widespread than they had expected. Counting all state legislatures together, those in favor of the amendment outvoted their opposition 5,084 to 1,265. Fully eighty percent of the representatives most responsive to the will of the people approved of prohibition.

Amendment backers were jubilant. On January 17, 1920—the day the amendment took effect—ten thousand prohibitionists celebrated with a mock funeral of John Barleycorn, an imaginary figure who symbolized the ill effects of alcohol. The funeral service was led by the Reverend Billy Sunday, a charismatic preacher and tireless backer of prohibition who had once been a professional baseball player. According to biographer Theodore Thomas Frankenberg, Sunday told his audience: "The reign of tears is over. The slums will soon be only a memory. We will turn our prisons into factories and our jails into storehouses and corn-cribs. Men will walk upright now, women will smile, and children will laugh. Hell will be forever for rent." Americans all over the country joined in anticipating a future free of the ill effects of alcohol.

Prohibition in Action

The next step for prohibitionists was to turn the amendment into law. Wayne Wheeler, a lawyer and prominent leader for the Anti-Saloon League, drafted a law called the National Prohibition Act. The law was introduced in the House by Andrew J. Volstead, and thus became known as the Volstead Act. According to Lucas, "One of the most controversial aspects of the Volstead Act was its definition of intoxicating beverages as any liquid containing more than half of one percent of alcohol. This came as a surprise to some who had supported prohibition, thinking it would be directly mainly at distilled liquors. They thought beer and wine would still be legal." Congress passed the law—over President Woodrow Wilson's veto—on October 27, 1919, and it went into effect at midnight on January 17, 1920, a year to the day after the passage of the amendment.

Prohibition backers boasted that within a year there would simply be no more alcohol in the nation. And for a brief time it seemed that Prohibition would work. One observer in New York, quoted in Eileen Lucas's *The Eighteenth and Twenty–First Amendments,* observed that "for a year or two [prohibition] was pretty generally observed and observed curiously enough because it did not occur to most people that it was possible to do anything else." Journalist Ida Tarbell traveled widely across the nation and claimed that "One sees liquor so rarely that you forget there is such a thing." But alcohol would not disappear so easily after all.

Enforcement and Resistance

The first signs of resistance to the Eighteenth Amendment came before and just after its passage, when a coalition of alcohol manufacturers, "personal liberty leagues," and lawyers protested that the amendment was unconstitutional. Eventually, the Supreme Court and lower courts heard seven cases that were presented together to the Supreme Court as the *National Prohibition Cases.* These cases claimed that the amendment was invalid, and they tried to stop enforcement of the Volstead Act. But the Supreme Court ruled that both the amendment and the Volstead Act were constitutional.

Federal enforcement of the Volstead Act was shared by the Justice Department, the Treasury Department's Prohibition Unit, and by state and local agencies. At first these forces merely had to make sure that saloons served no alcohol, not even watered down beer. But enforcement soon became more difficult in the face of widespread resistance and law-breaking.

DOCTOR, I NEED A DRINK! As soon as it became clear that Prohibition really would shut down American drinking establishments, Americans began devising ingenious ways to get their beloved drink. Some went to their doctors to get a prescription for alcohol; doctors gave out such prescriptions by the thousands. Others took to making alcohol at home, using home breweries to make beer or home stills to make hard liquor. One grape juice manufacturer provided instructions on the side of the bottle that instructed consumers not to let the juice sit in a cupboard for twenty–one days or it would turn into wine; people were all too ready to ignore this helpful warning.

SMUGGLING AND SPEAKEASIES. Law enforcement officials were unprepared for the amount of smuggling and illegal drinking that began to occur.

Eighteenth Amendment

Smugglers soon began to bring liquor across the border from Mexico, Canada, and the Bahamas. According to Lucas, "'Rum runners' brought liquor in boats from the British-controlled Bahama Islands to various places off the Atlantic coast. Bootleggers sailed out from the mainland to meet them. An especially notorious area for this exchange was along the Long Island, New York, and New Jersey shores. On some dark nights, there were as many as one hundred boats waiting for the illegal cargo." Law enforcement officials fought increasingly violent battles with these smugglers, and the newspapers loved to publish pictures of Prohibition agents smashing bottles of confiscated liquor. But the truth was that far more alcohol made it across the borders than was ever stopped.

Much of the smuggled and home-made alcohol made its way into the thousands of "speakeasies" that sprang up across the country, especially in big cities. A speakeasy was any place where illegal alcohol was served, and during Prohibition speakeasies took the place of saloons and bars. The jazz-influenced youth culture for which the 1920s is known flourished in the speakeasies: girls wore short dresses and short hair, couples danced the Charleston and the lindy, and booze flowed freely. Some of the alcohol served in speakeasies was "good"—made by reputable dis-

During prohibition, speakeasies sprung up all around the country. Reproduced by permission of Corbis-Bettmann.

tillers—but much of it was "bad"—brewed by amateurs, doctored with flavors, and sometimes downright poisonous. The downside of the speakeasies was that people sometimes died from drinking "bad" liquor. This danger may have added to the thrill of the speakeasy.

The Failure of Prohibition

By the mid-1920s one thing was clear: the Eighteenth Amendment and the laws designed to enforce it had not rid the nation of alcohol. Even worse, the amendment made criminals of all of those Americans who were unwilling to give up drinking. The profits to be made from the sale of alcohol soon encouraged the formation of an organized criminal element intent on controlling its distribution and sales. Moreover, the profitability of bootlegging (the illegal manufacture, transportation, or sale of alcohol) contributed to rampant bribery and corruption within law enforcement agencies. It seemed to many that the Eighteenth Amendment had created the very thing it had aimed to stop—damage to the social fabric of the nation.

During Prohibition some breweries started producing other products. Stroh's started producing ice cream. Reproduced by permission of AP/Wide World Photos.

Eighteenth Amendment

By the late 1920s enough people had become alarmed at the difficulties of enforcing the unpopular Prohibition laws that they began to propose that the Eighteenth Amendment be repealed. With the coming of the Great Depression (a severe economic downturn that began with the stock market crash of 1929) and the election of Franklin Delano Roosevelt in 1932, anti-Prohibitionists had gained enough support to win repeal through the passage of the Twenty–first Amendment on December 5, 1933.

The "noble experiment" that was the Eighteenth Amendment ended in failure. An attempt to enforce a code of moral conduct through the law had collided with Americans' desire to exercise their individual choice about personal behavior—and lost. Though Prohibition caused much social distress, it did reveal some real strengths in the Constitution, for it proved once again that the law of the land was able to be adapted to fit the changing needs of its people and that mistakes, once made, could in fact be corrected.

For More Information

Books

Barry, James P. *The Noble Experiment, 1919–1933: The Eighteenth Amendment Prohibits Liquor in America.* New York: Franklin Watts, 1972.

Beals, Carleton. *Cyclone Carry: The Story of Carry Nation.* Philadelphia: Chilton Co., 1962.

Behr, Edward. *Prohibition: Thirteen Years that Changed America.* New York: Arcade Publishing, 1996.

Bernstein, Richard B., with Jerome Agel. *Amending America: If We Love the Constitution So Much, Why Do We Keep Trying to Change It?* New York: Times Books/Random House, 1993; Lawrence: University Press of Kansas, 1995.

Cohen, Daniel. *Prohibition: America Makes Alcohol Illegal.* Brookfield, CT: Millbrook Press, 1995.

Hintz, Martin. *Farewell, John Barleycorn: Prohibition in the United States.* Minneapolis: Lerner Publications, 1996.

Kobler, John. *Ardent Spirits: The Rise and Fall of Prohibition.* New York: G. P. Putnam's Sons, 1973.

Kyvig, David E. *Repealing National Prohibition.* Chicago: The University of Chicago Press, 1979.

Kyvig, David E., editor. *Law, Alcohol, and Order: Perspectives on National Prohibition.* Westport, CT: Greenwood Press, 1985.

Eighteenth Amendment

Lucas, Eileen. *The Eighteenth and Twenty–First Amendments: Alcohol—Prohibition and Repeal.* Springfield, New Jersey: Enslow Publishers, 1998.

Rebman, Renee C. *Prohibition.* San Diego, CA: Lucent Books, 1998.

Rumbarger, John J. *Profits, Power, and Prohibition: Alcohol Reform and the Industrializing of America, 1800–1930.* Albany: State University of New York Press, 1989.

Sann, Paul. *The Lawless Decade.* New York: Crown, 1957.

Taylor, Robert Lewis. *Vessel of Wrath: The Life and Times of Carry Nation.* New York: New American Library, 1966.

Articles

American Museum. No. 4 (Philadelphia: Mathew Carey, 1788); reproduced in Richard B. Bernstein with Kym S. Rice, *Are We to Be a Nation? The Making of the Constitution.* Cambridge, MA: Harvard University Press, 1987.

Web Sites

"Carry Amelia Moore Nation." [Online] http://www.tsha.utexas.edu/handbook/online/articles/view/NN/fna7.html (accessed on August 3, 2000).

Kyvig, David. "Repealing National Prohibition." [Online] http://www.druglibrary.org/schaffer/history/rnp/rnptoc.htm (accessed on August 3, 2000).

"Temperance and Prohibition." [Online] http://www.history.ohio-state.edu/projects/prohibition/contents.htm (accessed August 2, 2000.)McWilliams, Peter. "Prohibition: A Lesson in the Futility (and Danger) of Prohibiting." [Online] http://www.mcwilliams.com/books/ aint/402.htm (accessed on August 3, 2000).

Nineteenth Amendment

The right of citizens of the United States to vote shall not be denied or abridged by the United States or any State on account of sex.

Congress shall have power to enforce this article by appropriate legislation.

The Nineteenth Amendment granted women the right to vote. Although a major victory for suffragists (supporters of a woman's right to vote), the amendment did not grant women all the rights they desired. Women continued to struggle for the right to participate more fully in the public realm long after the amendment was finally ratified on August 26, 1920, pushing for equal access to jobs and political power throughout the twentieth century.

Early Struggles

The Nineteenth Amendment addressed one part of a larger issue: the battle for women's rights. Throughout most of history, women experienced oppression and discrimination, giving them fewer opportunities than men to direct their own lives. Historically, custom and law kept women from owning property, holding some jobs, and speaking in public, among other things. Men traditionally dominated positions of political, economic, and religious power. Not only were women denied those positions, but they were also denied equal access to education. In the first half of the nineteenth century, "married women had no legal existence apart from their husbands; generally, women were uneducated and considered intellectually deficient," according to Judith Papachristou in *Women Together.* Women were to be seen and not heard. As women rebelled against this oppression, the women's rights movement was born.

RATIFICATION FACTS

PROPOSED: Submitted by Congress to the states on June 4, 1919.

RATIFICATION: Ratified by the required three-fourths of states (36 of 48) on August 18, 1920, and by twelve more states on March 22, 1984. Declared to be part of the Constitution on August 26, 1920.

RATIFYING STATES: Illinois, June 10, 1919 (and that State readopted its resolution of ratification June 17, 1919); Michigan, June 10, 1919; Wisconsin, June 10, 1919; Kansas, June 16, 1919; New York, June 16, 1919; Ohio, June 16, 1919; Pennsylvania, June 24, 1919; Massachusetts, June 25, 1919; Texas, June 28, 1919; Iowa, July 2, 1919; Missouri, July 3, 1919; Arkansas, July 28, 1919; Montana, August 2, 1919; Nebraska, August 2, 1919; Minnesota, September 8, 1919; New Hampshire, September 10, 1919; Utah, October 2, 1919; California, November 1, 1919; Maine, November 5, 1919; North Dakota, December 1, 1919; South Dakota, December 4, 1919; Colorado, December 15, 1919; Kentucky, January 6, 1920; Rhode Island, January 6, 1920; Oregon, January 13, 1920; Indiana, January 16, 1920; Wyoming, January 27, 1920; Nevada, February 7, 1920; New Jersey, February 9, 1920; Idaho, February 11, 1920; Arizona, February 12, 1920; New Mexico, February 21, 1920; Oklahoma, February 28, 1920; West Virginia, March 10, 1920; Washington, March 22, 1920; Tennessee, August 18, 1920.

Supporters of women's rights began to organize in the mid–1800s, at about the same time that the anti-slavery movement was gaining momentum in the North. At that time, only white men over twenty–one years old were considered "citizens" of the United States. Women believed that they would have a better chance of gaining rights for women if they pushed for rights for all people, including black slaves. In short, they hoped there would be strength in numbers.

A UNITED FRONT? There were tensions, however, between abolitionists (people who supported the end of slavery) and women's rights advocates. Although the founders of the women's rights movement were all abolitionists, not all of them believed in complete equality between men and women. Some feared that the push for equality at the ballot box might be too radical. They feared that the campaign for women's suffrage might

Soujourner Truth was an abolitionist as well as an advocate of women's rights. Courtesy of the Library of Congress.

jeopardize the push for equality in other areas, such as economic equality. Some abolitionists also feared that the fight to end slavery would be endangered by allowing women to speak from the abolitionist platform at a time when a woman's appearance in such a public forum was considered indecent. Both abolitionists and women's rights advocates worried that they were pushing too hard against social conventions.

The tension between both sides of the movement for civil rights reached a high point when women delegates to the "World's Anti-slavery Convention" in 1840—held in London—were not allowed to participate. Such divisiveness grew between the women and the abolitionists that they failed to form a united front against discrimination.

SENECA FALLS. After their failure to participate in the World's Anti-slavery Convention, women's rights advocates realized they needed to rethink their approach. In 1848, Elizabeth Cady Stanton, Lucretia Mott, and several others called a meeting in Seneca Falls, New York. Most historians trace the early formation of the suffragist movement to this date, when three hundred men and women congregated in Seneca Falls to protest the inferior status of women. Believing that the time was right to advocate their cause separately from the abolitionists, Stanton, Mott, and the others drafted the *Seneca Falls Declaration of Sentiments,* which outlined how women were oppressed. Stanton also wrote resolutions to implement the *Declaration.* The resolutions addressed gaining personal freedom, the

ability to own property, the ability to testify in court, and access to education and employment, among other things. The only resolution that was not unanimously adopted was one that promoted women's suffrage.

Civil War Blues

Though the Civil War (1861–65) brought sweeping social and political changes to the United States, it proved disappointing in terms of the progress of the women's rights movement. After the Seneca Falls convention, no additional women's rights conventions were held until the end of the war. Women who, during the war, had worked to support the war effort hoped that they could use

Elizabeth Cady Stanton was one of the organizers of the convention at Seneca Falls. Courtesy of the National Archives and Records Administration.

this fact to their advantage in peacetime. In 1866, suffragists rejoined with abolitionists to propose a constitutional amendment that prohibited voter discrimination based on gender. But the Republican Party declared that "this is the Negro's hour" and promptly shut the door on women trying to build momentum for federal female suffrage.

A DIVIDED FRONT. The adoption of the Fourteenth Amendment in 1868 did little to strengthen the movement for women's rights. Although the amendment expanded the definition of the word "citizen" to include blacks, it also introduced the word "male" into the Constitution for the first time. Some women argued that the amendment should be defeated; others argued that even if they had not yet gained equal rights, it was no reason for blacks not to get theirs. The passage of the Fifteenth Amend-

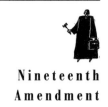

The efforts of Susan B. Anthony in the fight for women's suffrage are honored by the Susan B. Anthony silver dollar. Reproduced by permission of Eastword Publications Development.

ment, which gave blacks the right to vote, also angered some women's rights advocates.

Divisiveness over the Fourteenth and Fifteenth Amendments grew among suffragists until they split to form two separate organizations in 1869: the American Woman Suffrage Association and the National Woman Suffrage Association (led by Stanton and Susan B. Anthony). The American Woman Suffrage Association pursued state suffrage amendments and smaller-scale changes to effect women's right to vote. The National Woman Suffrage Association rallied behind the idea of a constitutional amendment and promoted more confrontational methods of campaigning. The division between the two groups lasted until 1890, when the two organizations merged, largely due to the efforts of Stanton and Anthony, into the National American Woman Suffrage Association (NAWSA). Reunited with the others, the NAWSA began to pursue suffrage at the state level and made federal suffrage a secondary goal.

Actual Progress?

The years between the end of the Civil War and 1890, when the NWSA and the AWSA worked for women's suffrage in different ways, saw significant progress. Stanton and Anthony and the NWSA continued to push

ELIZABETH CADY STANTON

Elizabeth Cady Stanton (1815–1902) was the driving force behind the first women's rights convention in 1848. Born into a wealthy family in Johnstown, New York, Stanton had resolved early in life to become an advocate for women's rights. After receiving an education at the Troy Female Seminary in New York, one of the first women's academies to offer an advanced education similar to male academies, Stanton began to observe her father's work as a judge and lawyer. During this time she witnessed firsthand the legal discrimination that women suffered — learning, among other things, that women had no legal protection from being beaten by their husbands and had no legal claim to their own children. She also witnessed the discrimination of women when, during her honeymoon, she attempted to participate in the World Anti-Slavery Convention in 1840 but learned women were not allowed to participate. In addition, she experienced discrimination and hardship in her struggle to raise her five children with little help from her husband, Henry B. Stanton, who spent much of his time away from home.

Stanton had met Lucretia Mott at the World Anti-Slavery Convention. Over the years, the two kept in touch and fostered the idea of a women's convention. By 1848, Stanton was ready. Stanton and Mott, with three other women, crafted the *Seneca Falls Declaration of Senti-*

for a federal amendment for women's suffrage. During these years, they tried to win women's suffrage through the courts—with little success. But the NWSA attracted the most attention when it organized women to register to vote and made special ballot boxes to hold women's votes in the 1872 presidential election. Anthony was arrested for casting a vote in this election and was fined $100, which she refused to pay. In 1878, Congress finally entertained the first woman suffrage proposal; a similar version of the proposal (sometimes called the "Susan B. Anthony Amendment") was passed nearly 40 years later.

During the same period, the AWSA gained considerable ground. Women in New York State were given the right to sole possession of what they owned before they married—even though they still could not give it away as inheritance. Kansas was the first in a string of states to allow women to vote in school elections in the 1860s (though Kentucky

ments, which detailed what they called the "absolute tyranny" men had over women. Though the *Declaration of Sentiments* met with public ridicule, it helped convince more and more women to join the ranks of the women's rights movement.

In 1851, Stanton met another figure who significantly influenced her views: Susan B. Anthony. Stanton and Anthony started the *Revolution* newspaper together and worked together as women's rights advocates for the next 50 years. Stanton and Anthony organized the National Woman Suffrage Association (NWSA) in 1869, and Stanton served as president for nearly twenty years. When the NWSA merged with a more conservative women's group in 1890 to become the National American Woman Suffrage Association, Stanton was elected president. But Stanton's public criticism of organized religion and of the Bible eventually robbed her of her leadership role in the organization. Stanton's publication of *The Women's Bible* (1895 and another edition in 1898), often described as "a study of sexism in the Old Testament," sealed her fate as an outcast in the movement she had started. In *The Women's Bible* Stanton argued against the subordination of women in society. The protest surrounding this work was too much for many of her colleagues to stomach and they condemned her. Although Elizabeth Cady Stanton died in 1902 before she could see the ratification of the Nineteenth Amendment, her earlier work was instrumental to the amendment's ultimate victory.

had become the first state to allow school suffrage in 1831). By 1890, fifteen other states followed suit.

Wider forms of suffrage continued to be introduced, and by 1887 women had been granted municipal suffrage (the right to vote in city elections) in Kansas. Even more progressive than this, though, was Wyoming's declaration of full political equality for women and others in 1869. In fact, Wyoming was the first state to enter the Union, in 1890, with full suffrage for women. Although Colorado followed in 1893 and Utah in 1896, there would be a long wait before other states would extend suffrage to women.

In addition, despite considerable resistance, more and more women were making their way into the public realm. The number of women in American colleges rose significantly, as did the number of women employed in factories. These gains provided momentum to suffragists.

By 1890 the NWSA and the AWSA reunited as the National American Woman Suffrage Association (NAWSA). The newly-united group focused primarily on gaining suffrage at the state level, but did not abandon the secondary goal of federal suffrage.

Beyond the "Doldrums"

Although the NAWSA campaigned vigorously, it did not win victories in any new states from 1896 to 1910. These years would later be called the "doldrums." Even though women failed to make progress toward suffrage for nearly fourteen years, they did not quit. Instead, they continued to plan for the future and lobbied for women's suffrage throughout the country. By 1908, the NAWSA had begun collecting signatures to persuade President Theodore Roosevelt (served 1901–1909) to support women's suffrage. The NAWSA had more than 400,000 signatures within two years, and, in 1912, Roosevelt made women's suffrage a part of his unsuccessful campaign to regain the White House.

In 1919, The Equality League held the first suffrage parade in New York City. The event was quite a shock for many New Yorkers, but it quickly proved effective for the suffragists and became an annual event in many other cities; the parades were a perfect way to publicize their cause. By 1910 and 1911, significant victories occurred in the states of Washington and California, respectively. Other close losses left hope that more victories were close at hand. Also encouraging were the number of new suffragists from the South, a region that had been slow to mobilize around the issue during the nineteenth century.

By 1910, the suffrage movement had gained momentum again. In the years after 1910, many new suffrage groups sprang up, and organizations like churches and labor unions began to back the cause. The suffrage movement also benefited from the increasing number of women who had earned a college degree. These women were highly motivated and offered a breath of fresh air to the ranks. By "1916 there were 41 state amendment campaigns, with 9 victories and 32 defeats," according to Aileen S. Kraditor, as quoted in *The Ideas of the Woman Suffrage Movement: 1890-1920.*

Progress Equals Unity?

Although significant progress was being made towards the enfranchisement of women, the NAWSA continued to be plagued by factionalism

*Alice Paul was a
part of a new
generation of
suffragists. She was
more highly
educated and had
the motivation of the
women who went
before her boosting
her up.* Courtesy of the
Library of Congress.

(disagreement among different groups within the movement). In 1913, members of NAWSA formed a Congressional Union for Woman Suffrage (CU) to pursue a federal amendment for women's voting rights. Although a women's voting rights amendment had been proposed at each session of Congress since the later part of the nineteenth century, it had not been debated in either House since 1887. That all changed with the determination of Alice Paul and Lucy Burns, who headed NAWSA's Congressional Committee (which became the CU).

SUSAN B. ANTHONY

Susan B. Anthony (1820–1906) was as ardent in the fight for women's suffrage as her longtime friend Elizabeth Cady Stanton. Anthony worked much of her adult life for women's rights.

Born in Massachusetts to a father who was a Quaker Abolitionist, Anthony had moral zeal in her blood. Early in life, she directed this reformist energy toward the abolition of slavery and liquor; eventually applying it to the fight for women's rights with equal fervor. In 1872, calling for the same civil rights afforded blacks under the Fourteenth and Fifteenth Amendments, Anthony led a group of women to the ballot box in Rochester, New York, to test the right to vote. Her arrest two weeks later did nothing to slow her down and she continued to lecture for women's rights. In 1873 she once again tried to vote in city elections. Charged with and convicted of breaking the voting laws, Anthony refused to pay her fine. Indeed, she said she would stop at nothing short of a federal amendment.

Anthony's devotion to the cause of gaining a federal suffrage amendment, a cause she saw as key to the emancipation of women, marks her as perhaps the greatest member of the suffrage movement. She lectured throughout the country on women's rights and her organizational skills were unparalleled in the women's movement. By 1888, she had organized the International Council of Women, and when, in 1904, she had organized the International Woman Suffrage Alliance, Anthony was already revered worldwide for her contributions to the cause of women's rights. Anthony devoted her life to her advocacy. When Stanton resigned, in 1892, as president of the NAWSA amidst the controversy of her radical views, the 72-year-old Anthony took over. Unfortunately, Susan B. Anthony did not live to see the fruits of her work realized with passage of the Nineteenth Amendment. She died in her home in 1906.

MARCHING FOR CHANGE. Paul and Burns chose one of the most public forums to get their message out: a women's march held on the day before Woodrow Wilson's inauguration as president in 1913. Many who had gathered for the presidential celebration were not amused, and a riot soon broke out requiring the use of troops to restore quiet. The women had gained the attention they desired!

The women continued their political campaign with a march on Capitol Hill on the first day of a special session of Congress. This was followed with demonstrations in various states and then with a petition to the Senate. The tactics proved successful and, in 1913, the amendment was debated in Congress for the first time in twenty-six years. Though passage of the amendment was still some years away, new life had been breathed into the suffrage movement.

Paul and Burns decided that they were too close to victory to risk having the suffrage issue placed on the back burner again. To ensure that this momentum would not be lost, they formed the Congressional Union in 1913, an organization with the sole aim of passing the federal amendment. All was not smooth sailing from this point on, however. Factionalism once again threatened any unity the movement had found in its recent success. Divisions grew between women supporting the aggressive tactics of the CU and the gentler and more conservative tactics of the NAWSA. The two groups split in 1914.

Nineteenth Amendment

The Progressive Era

Women certainly benefited from the politics of the Progressive Era (roughly 1900 to 1920), a time in American political history when many people united to give citizens more control over their public and private lives. The Sixteenth Amendment, which established a federal income tax, the Seventeenth Amendment, which established the direct election of senators, and the Nineteenth Amendment are called "Progressive" amendments because they were passed during this era when reformers rallied the public to make radical changes in the government.

NEW WAYS TO USE AMENDMENTS. The passage of the Sixteenth and the Seventeenth Amendments in 1913 ushered in a wave of new thinking about the purpose of constitutional amendments. During the forty years following the Civil War when no constitutional amendments were ratified, politicians and social advocates had begun to question the usefulness of the Constitution, thinking it seemed too inflexible to address changing social realities. Though hundreds of amendments had been proposed during these forty years, none could gain the two-thirds majority in the Congressional houses needed to send them to be ratified by three-fourths of the states. But when, in 1913, enough consensus was

Nineteenth Amendment

Alice Paul and Lucy Burns, leaders of the National Woman's Party, picketing outside the White House in 1917. Courtesy of the Library of Congress.

developed to ratify two constitutional amendments in the same year, the process of amending the Constitution began to seem like a more realistic solution to a variety of social and political problems. The American public recognized the power of constitutional amendments to redirect the activities of government. Perhaps more importantly, they also realized their own power, through the amendment process, to change the Constitution to create a government that was responsive to their needs and desires.

Progressive advocates succeeded in passing amendments designed to wrest the control of government from large corporations and to grant that control to the people. Constitutional amendments seemed like good ways to restrict alcohol use, regulate child labor, and finally to grant voting rights for women. The Progressive Era's attention to the family (alcohol abuse was seen as a blight on the family) and children gave women more political significance than ever before. Many Americans believed that women were the carriers of virtue, so it only made sense that they be allowed further access to the public community to change it for the better. Women used these changing views about their public role to their advantage, and began to make real gains in their push for suffrage. In

addition, Progressive Party members, male and female, rallied around the idea of a more inclusive democracy that incorporated women into the voting public.

Carrie Chapman Catt's push to turn the NAWSA's attention toward federal suffrage was the key to the amendment finally being drafted. Courtesy of the Library of Congress.

We Want Attention!

So determined were advocates for women's suffrage that even a World War would not stop them. For years, suffragists had attempted to win an audience with the president to discuss the voting issue, but without any success. Unwilling to put aside their suffrage goals during World War I (1914–17), the CU continued plans to get the president's attention. When the CU merged with the Woman's Party (WP) in 1917, members of the WP began picketing the White House.

People were not used to seeing picketers outside the chief executive's mansion. Two teams of "silent sentinels" stood at the White House gates every day for a year and a half, holding banners that demanded the vote. As World War I raged on and the picketers continued to stand on the sidewalks outside the White House demanding women's suffrage, onlookers and police who at first had been curious and bemused became insulting and vicious. As the WP picketers silently held their banners and signs, they were assaulted and harassed. Although those who hit them and tore their banners were not arrested, the picketers were. In prison, the women went on hunger strikes and were brutally force-fed by the police.

Nineteenth Amendment

CARRIE CHAPMAN CATT

Carrie Chapman Catt (1859–1947) devised the strategy that eventually won women the right to vote. Catt had served as president of the National American Woman Suffrage Association (NAWSA) from 1900 to 1904 and resumed her leadership in 1915. She was also one of the first female school superintendents in the country.

When Catt resumed presidency of the NAWSA she refocused the organization's efforts on obtaining a federal amendment. Catt also believed strongly in the notion that women's participation in the public sphere could help solve America's problems. She argued that women were a big part of the solution since they cared most about the good of society. Catt predicted that her "Winning Plan," which detailed a strategy for gaining state and presidential support for women's suffrage, would take several years to complete.

Catt mobilized women around the notion of taking household issues into the public sphere. Because of their experience in the home, she argued, women were in a good position to push for legislation about such things as protecting children in the workplace and ensuring safety standards for food and drugs. Women could also deal with hous-

All in all, 218 women were arrested and 97 were sent to jail. Although the courts invalidated all of the sentences, the episodes painted an ugly picture of what could happen to democracy at home if it were not watched over vigilantly.

The Final Stretch

While the WP brought public attention to the efforts of women suffragists, the NAWSA brought the women's rights movement respectability. The NAWSA had quietly supported the war effort while the WP picketed, trying to keep its efforts dignified and distancing itself from the radical WP. Many of its members went to work in jobs once held by men, and spent many hours in public service. Although the WP never had as many members as the NAWSA, the two groups were both effective in blazing the trail toward the federal amendment.

ing issues because they brought with them some basic knowledge that men lacked.

Catt thought women could only effect real change in their lives and in the country with political power: the power to vote. While Catt crusaded for women to gain a political voice, however, she was opposed to equal rights for women. An Equal Rights Amendment, she argued, would expose women to danger rather than protecting them from it. Because women were different from men, they needed safeguards in the public realm; after all, women get pregnant and cannot work fourteen-hour days. Gender distinctions, in her opinion, needed to be maintained. Although she recognized differences between men and women, Catt was equally ardent about the fact that differences should not be translated as weaknesses.

After helping to secure women's suffrage, Catt turned in the 1920s to the peace movement. In 1925, she brought together eleven national women's organizations to form the Committee on the Cause and Cure of War, the largest women's peace group of that decade. Following World War II, Catt turned her interest to the United Nations and used her influence to place women on various commissions. She continued to work for peace and social justice until she died in 1947.

Carrie Chapman Catt was instrumental in orchestrating the strategy that would finally result in a federal amendment. In 1915, Catt, past president of the NAWSA, once again took up the reins of leadership and pushed the NAWSA to turn its attention from state to federal suffrage. By 1917, Catt had reorganized the NAWSA into a smoothly–running political machine, ready to join other organizations in the fight for a federal amendment.

The first step was to use the lessons of Paul and Burns by holding rallies and parades in order to gain publicity. Unlike the WP, however, the NAWSA decided against a combative strategy and instead concentrated on persuasion and public education. Indeed, Catt was a master politician who knew how to work for gradual, but lasting, change.

Convincing a president NAWSA members remained nonpartisan in an attempt to gain support from a wider base and to distance themselves from the bad taste of the confrontations that had occurred in front of the

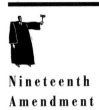

Nineteenth Amendment

White House. The strategy was effective, and the NAWSA eventually convinced President Wilson that it was politically beneficial to support a federal amendment.

In 1918, Wilson asked Congress to consider a suffrage amendment. On January 10, 1918, the House passed the amendment. The next step was to bring it before the Senate, and Wilson himself decided to appear in support of it. Despite Wilson's support, the amendment failed by two votes. It was clear, however, that it was only a matter of time before it passed. The momentum was too great to prevent it. Finally, on June 4, 1919, Congress approved the Nineteenth Amendment. It was ratified by the states and officially became a part of the Constitution on August 26, 1920.

Women have come a long way since the struggle for suffrage. Geraldine Ferraro ran as the first ever female vice-presidential nominee for a major party in 1984. Reproduced by permission of Archive Photos, Inc.

Conclusion

After more than seventy years of relentless work, women finally won the vote. What began as a small meeting of a handful of women ended in a massive political movement supported by millions. Although the movement was fraught with factionalism, in the end it was the work of all sides that resulted in the adoption of the Nineteenth Amendment into the Constitution of the United States of America.

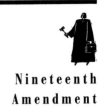

From the beginning, however, the struggle was about much more than the right to vote. More importantly, it was about a change in roles for women in the public realm. No longer did men control this domain exclusively. All is not yet finished in the struggle for equality between the sexes; there is still room for more political activism, and for equality in wages. This chapter in the battle, however, proved that women have played and continue to play a significant role in U.S. history.

Unlike other amendments, the Nineteenth Amendment has received few challenges or reinterpretations from the courts. The single greatest challenge to the amendment—posed by states which had not ratified the amendment and wished to continue to deprive women of the right to vote—was resolved by the Supreme Court in the 1922 case of *Leser v. Garnett,* which declared that the amendment was binding to every state.

Elizabeth Dole threw her hat in the race for the Republican candidate for presidency in 1999.
Reproduced by permission of AP/Wide World Photos.

For More Information

Books

Burby, Liza N. *Leaders of Women's Suffrage.* San Diego, CA: Lucent Books, 1998.

Cott, Nancy F. *A Woman Making History: Mary Ritter Beard Through Her Letters.* New Haven, Connecticut: Yale University Press, 1991.

Nineteenth Amendment

Kraditor, Aileen S. *The Ideas of the Woman Suffrage Movement: 1890–1920.* New York: Doubleday & Company, Inc., 1971.

Monroe, Judy. *The Nineteenth Amendment: Women's Right to Vote.* Berkeley Heights, New Jersey: Enslow, 1998.

Papachristou, Judith. *Women Together: A History in Documents of the Women's Movement in the United States.* New York: Alfred A. Knopf, 1976.

Stalcup, Brenda. *Women's Suffrage.* San Diego, California: Greenhaven Press, 2000.

Stanton, Elizabeth Cady, et al. *The Woman's Bible.* 2 vols. New York: European Publishing Company, 1895 and 1898.

Stein, R. Conrad. *The Story of the Nineteenth Amendment.* Danbury, Connecticut: Children's Press, 1982.

Turoff, Barbara K. *Mary Beard as Force in History.* Dayton, Ohio: Wright State University Press, 1979.

Weatherford, Doris. *A History of the American Suffragist Movement.* Santa Barbara, California: ABC-Clio, 1998.

Web Sites

"Elizabeth Cady Stanton." [Online] http://www.nps.gov/wori/ecs.htm (accessed on 12 June 2000).

"Encyclopedia of Women in American Politics." [Online] http://www.political-landscape.com/women/toc.html (accessed 13 June 2000).

"Motherhood, Social Service, and Political Reform: Political Culture and Imagery of American Women Suffrage." [Online] http://www.nmwh.org/exhibits/exhibit_frames.html (accessed 25 July 2000).

"The Nineteenth Amendment." [Online] http://www.nara.gov/exhall/charters/constitution/19th/html (accessed 12 June 2000).

"Susan B. Anthony Biography." [Online] http://www.susanbanthonyhouse.org/biography.html (accessed 13 June 2000).

"Votes for Women." [Online] http://www.huntington.org/vfw/main.html (accessed 25 July 2000).

"The War, Civil Disobedience, and the Nineteenth Amendment." [Online] http://www.san-marino.k12.ca.us/~heh/thepagex?chap9.html (accessed 15 June 2000.)"Winning the Right to Vote." [Online] http://www.greatwomen.org/lcvt.htm (accessed 15 June 2000).

"Woman Suffrage and the 19th Amendment: Primary Sources, Activities, and Links to Related Web Sites for Educators and Students." [Online] http://www.nara.gov/education/teaching/woman/home.html (accessed July 25, 2000.)

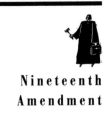

Nineteenth Amendment

Twentieth Amendment

SECTION 1. The terms of the President and Vice President shall end at noon on the 20th day of January, and the terms of Senators and Representatives at noon on the 3d day of January, of the years in which such terms would have ended if this article had not been ratified; and the terms of their successors shall then begin.

SECTION 2. The Congress shall assemble at least once in every year, and such meeting shall begin at noon on the 3d day of January, unless they shall by law appoint a different day.

SECTION 3. If, at the time fixed for the beginning of the term of the President, the President elect shall have died, the Vice President elect shall become President. If a President shall not have been chosen before the time fixed for the beginning of his term, or if the President elect shall have failed to qualify, then the Vice President elect shall act as President until a President shall have qualified; and the Congress may by law provide for the case wherein neither a President elect nor a Vice President elect shall have qualified, declaring who shall then act as President, or the manner in which one who is to act shall be selected, and such person shall act accordingly until a President or Vice President shall have qualified.

SECTION 4. The Congress may by law provide for the case of death of any of the persons from whom the House of Representatives may choose a President whenever the right of choice shall have devolved upon them, and for the case of the death of any of the persons from whom the Senate may choose a Vice President whenever the right of choice shall have devolved upon them.

SECTION 5. Sections 1 and 2 shall take effect on the 15th day of October following the ratification of this article.

SECTION 6. This article shall be inoperative unless it shall have been ratified as an amendment to the Constitution by the legislatures of three-fourths of the several States within seven years from the date of its submission.

T o a great extent, the Twentieth Amendment was meant to simplify and clarify election procedures that had, by the twentieth century, become outdated. When the Constitution was first adopted, a new Congress needed plenty of time between an election (conducted in November) and the actual commencement of work. With rapid changes in transportation and communication in the twentieth century, however, election results are quickly known and legislators can travel from anywhere in the United States to the nation's capital in a short amount of time. This amendment thus shortened the time between the election and the beginning of the Congressional term.

Additionally, the amendment was a serious attempt to address the issue of presidential succession. An essential element of any democratic country is the peaceful and smooth transfer of power. The Twentieth Amendment, then, aimed at resolving the confusion that might arise if no presidential candidate in an election year received a majority of electoral votes. If this were to happen, the amendment specified that the old Congress, and not the newly- elected one, would choose the new president.

The Twentieth Amendment is often referred to as the "lame duck" amendment because of sections one and two, which move the presidential inauguration date from March 4 to January 20, move the start of the Congressional term to January 3, and require Congress to meet at least once a year. Under the original terms of our Constitution, the terms of members of the House and one-third of the members of the Senate expired on the fourth day of March. This required the departing Congress to meet in a short session in which little was ever accomplished. Moving the date on which Congress convenes to January 3 was intended to give representatives plenty of time to address general legislation. In effect, the amendment ended the so-called short session of Congress.

Why January?

As you have watched presidents, vice presidents, and other elected officials shiver through lengthy inaugural ceremonies you may have wondered: Why is the President's inauguration always held in the cold month of January? In truth, the date has nothing to do with weather and everything to do with providing for more effective government. The Twentieth Amendment moved the date of inauguration from a spring-like March 4 to a wintry January 20 in order to place elected officials more quickly into the offices for which they were selected. The amendment was ratified in 1933, took effect in 1937, and people have been braving the cold ever since.

RATIFICATION FACTS

PROPOSED: Submitted by Congress to the states on March 2, 1932.

RATIFICATION: Ratified by the required three-fourths of states (36 of 48) on January 23, 1933, and by the remaining 12 states on April 26, 1933. Declared to be part of the Constitution on February 6, 1933.

RATIFYING STATES: Virginia, March 4, 1932; New York, March 11, 1932; Mississippi, March 16, 1932; Arkansas, March 17, 1932; Kentucky, March 17, 1932; New Jersey, March 21, 1932; South Carolina, March 25, 1932; Michigan, March 31, 1932; Maine, April 1, 1932; Rhode Island, April 14, 1932; Illinois, April 21, 1932; Louisiana, June 22, 1932; West Virginia, July 30, 1932; Pennsylvania, August 11, 1932; Indiana, August 15, 1932; Texas, September 7, 1932; Alabama, September 13, 1932; California, January 4, 1933; North Carolina, January 5, 1933; North Dakota, January 9, 1933; Minnesota, January 12, 1933; Arizona, January 13, 1933; Montana, January 13, 1933; Nebraska, January 13, 1933; Oklahoma, January 13, 1933; Kansas, January 16, 1933; Oregon, January 16, 1933; Delaware, January 19, 1933; Washington, January 19, 1933; Wyoming, January 19, 1933; Iowa, January 20, 1933; South Dakota, January 20, 1933; Tennessee, January 20, 1933; Idaho, January 21, 1933; New Mexico, January 21, 1933; Georgia, January 23, 1933; Missouri, January 23, 1933; Ohio, January 23, 1933; Utah, January 23, 1933.

The first presidential inauguration was actually held in a warmer month: April 30, 1789. Following the first inauguration, the date for a new president's inauguration was set as March 4, and remained there until 1937. In 1792, the year Congress set the March 4 date, the interval between the date of a November election and the commencement of service made perfect sense. The lack of modern means of communication and transportation meant that time was needed for election results to be made public and for newly-elected officials to make the journey to the nation's capital.

With the Twentieth Amendment, however, the interval between the November election and the end of a president's term in March was shortened. By moving the end date from March 4 to January 20 (January 3, in the case of Congress), proponents of the amendment hoped to end the "lame duck" syndrome (see sidebar). Thus, the Twentieth Amendment is often referred to as the "lame duck" Amendment.

Changing Demands on the Federal Government

During the early nineteenth century the federal government was far less involved in shaping the political life of America than it is today. Because of its limited powers, the fact that there were no laws requiring Congress to meet a certain number of times each year did not pose a serious problem. In fact, Americans at this time were still somewhat suspicious of a government that appeared too intrusive in states' political affairs.

As the country grew through the nineteenth century and the federal government expanded to take on more responsibilities, the idea of a "part-time" government that met inconsistently was clearly no longer feasible. Although major changes would not come until the early days of the twentieth century, the disadvantages of things like long and short congressional sessions was becoming clear. Congress usually conducted two sessions, a longer one that began a year and month after the November election and a shorter one beginning in the December immediately after the election and lasting until March 3, when it expired. One of the more obvious problems caused by this practice was the fact that each new Congress did not actually meet for over a year after its election by the people. The only exception to this was if the president used his constitutional power to call Congress into special session, as happened in 1861 after the outbreak of the Civil War.

The fact that Congress was unavailable in times of crisis, unless the president summoned its members, was a serious threat to the stability of the Union. More troubling yet was the fact that for thirteen months there was no speaker of the house or president pro tempore because the presiding officers of the Congress could not be chosen until the first "regular" session actually convened. If something happened to the president and vice president during the thirteen-month period when the presiding officers of the Congress had not yet been chosen, there would have been no one available to act as president despite the 1792 law governing presidential succession. In fact, there were several occasions during the nineteenth century when the vice president died in office and there was neither a speaker of the house nor a senate president pro tempore. These types of potential crises would force the federal government to define more clearly its role in guiding the growth of the Union.

WHAT IS THE "LAME DUCK" SYNDROME?

Originating in the mid-1700s, the term "lame duck" applies to an elected official who has not been reelected but still holds office. For example, when presidents have already served their maximum two terms or are defeated in a bid for reelection, they nevertheless remain in office after the election in November, serving until the president-elect is inaugurated in January. This interval is the lame duck period. Early in U.S. history this lag between the election and the swearing-in of officials was almost a necessity given slow means of transportation and communication. In fact, once the November election was set, it was more than a year before newly elected Congressmen met in December.

Officials on their way out were often referred to as lame ducks because it was thought that they could accomplish very little between the election and the end of their terms. Given the cumbersome nature of the legislative process, many felt that their authority had been severely challenged either by the voters or by the approaching end of their natural terms. Additionally, Congress was much less likely to support an outgoing president's policy initiatives, and a returning president was not as likely to sign off on laws sent by a Congress whose majority may have shifted as the result of an election.

The first major illustration of the direct problems resulting from lame-duck congresses and presidents came in early 1801. Federalists lost control of both houses of Congress and the presidency in the election of 1800, but the old Sixth Congress was still in power until March 3, 1801. The problem came when Republican Thomas Jefferson and Federalist Aaron Burr tied in Electoral College votes in their run for the presidency.

THE SALARY GRAB ACT. An even more pressing problem resulted when lame-duck Congresses passed bills that had little merit or granted favors to members of the House or Senate who were on their way out. One of the better-known examples of this occurred on March 3, 1873, when the Forty-second Congress attempted to raise their salaries by an exorbitant amount. The act quickly became know as the Salary Grab Act because of its measure raising congressional salaries from $5,000 per year to $7,500 per year. Furthermore, the act made the increase retroactive to the beginning of the session, meaning that each representative and senator, includ-

As specified by the Constitution, the electoral deadlock was to be broken by the House of Representatives. But it would not be the new House elected in 1800 as part of the Seventh Congress that would break the deadlock, but rather the rejected Federalist majority of the Sixth Congress that would decide whether it was to be Jefferson or Burr who would become president. Though Jefferson eventually won the decision, it took thirty-six ballots and two weeks before he was finally named president.

Another famous problem resulting from the lame duck period was illustrated in the *Marbury v. Madison* case in 1803. The case arose in response to lame-duck appointments made by outgoing president John Adams—who had a habit of making a series of late-night, last-minute appointments—and set the stage for a landmark Supreme Court decision. This decision, written by Chief Justice John Marshall, denied the appointment made by lame-duck president Adams by declaring an earlier act of Congress relating to such appointments unconstitutional. This landmark ruling—the first time the Supreme Court declared an act of Congress unconstitutional—established the Court as an equal partner in federal government.

In the end, the Twentieth Amendment cleared up the problem of lame-duck appointments by shortening the lame duck period. The Congress is now sworn in on January 3 following the election, and the president is sworn in on January 20. Although the amendment came to be known as the "lame duck" amendment, it also closed the gap in presidential power by specifying what will happen if a president-elect dies before being sworn in, and reduced the awkward period during which an outgoing president holds office.

ing the ones on their way out of office at the end of the session, received $5,000 in back pay—$2,500 per year for the previous two years.

In the end, many members of both houses of Congress attempted to compensate for their poor judgment in adopting the Salary Grab Act. Some even donated their money to charities, and others returned the money directly to the federal treasury. Neither these acts nor the Congressional repeal of the act in January 1874 did much to placate the public's anger. Driven by a strong distrust of their elected officials, many citizens ousted those involved in the scandal in the 1874 Congressional

elections. The event, once again, clearly illustrated the problems with the lame duck period.

Reformers to the Rescue!

Reform, however, was not far away. The twentieth century brought with it an intense push for a change in the way the federal government conducted its business. Few amendments can be traced to one legislator, but,

Senator George W. Norris was the author of the Twentieth Amendment. Courtesy of the Library of Congress.

to a large degree, the Twentieth Amendment came about as the result of the perseverance of one man: Senator George W. Norris (see sidebar on page 396). Indeed, as early as 1923 Norris became interested in the idea of a lame duck amendment and he would not turn back until he saw the idea come into fruition.

Norris was first elected to the United States House of Representatives in 1904 and quickly earned a reputation as a man of conscience. From the beginning of his career, he often found himself at odds with his colleagues over the bills he supported. During his fifth term in office, for example, Norris began a campaign to limit the autocratic powers of the speaker of the house who, up until 1910, enjoyed full control of the flow of all bills introduced in the House. In 1912 Norris won election to the Senate and he spent the next thirty years of his life using his position to improve the lives of farmers and the working poor.

Norris was a prominent member of the Progressive branch of the Republican Party. The Progressives believed that government needed to be more responsive to the needs of ordinary citizens, and they spearheaded many of the reforms that are associated with the Progressive Era in American politics. During the 1920s Norris turned his attention to adopting the lame duck amendment to the Constitution. The amendment, written and sponsored by Norris, was eventually adopted and applied to both houses of Congress as well as to the pPresident and vice president, but not before considerable controversy.

Political Passion and the Road to the Twentieth Amendment

Norris first became interested in a lame-duck amendment after witnessing the controversy over a 1922 bill, supported by then-President Warren G. Harding, that expanded the government's commitment to the construction of ships. In spite of the controversy surrounding the subsidy bill, Harding used his political influence to push it through a lame-duck Congress supported, of course, by Congressmen who had already been voted out of office several weeks before voting on the bill.

Senator Thaddeus Caraway, a Democrat from Arkansas, was enraged at these actions and sponsored a resolution barring lame-duck Congressmen from participating in the making of federal law. Although the resolution was highly unpopular, it was referred to the Senate Committee on Agriculture and Forestry, chaired by Norris. After spending

GEORGE W. NORRIS: POLITICAL LEGEND FROM NEBRASKA

The driving force behind the creation of the Twentieth Amendment, George W. Norris (1861–1944) was a celebrated senator from Nebraska known for obeying his conscience rather than the commands of political parties. Born in Sandusky, Ohio, in 1861 to a farming family, Norris lost his father and older brother when he was only three years old and, as a result, grew up in near poverty. After earning a law degree from Northern Indiana Normal School, Norris headed west, eventually settling in Nebraska. Over the next several years, the future Senator built a success-ful law practice, married and had three children, and began to gain wealth through speculation in land. In 1892 Norris had his first taste of public life when he was elected prosecuting attorney for Furnas County. Three years later he was elected district judge to Nebraska's Fourteenth District.

Norris was first elected to the United States House of Representa-tives in 1904 and joined the Senate beginning in 1912. As an influential member of the Republican party's Progressive branch, Norris was instrumental in the passage of progressive legislation during the 1910s and early 1920s. According to his autobiography, *Fighting Liberal,* his decade-long quest to secure passage of the Twentieth Amendment was one of the most grueling challenges of his career, but it was certainly not his last. Norris was also known for his sponsorship of legislation

time reviewing the proposal and the issues surrounding lame-duck elected officials, Norris became convinced that something had to be done. In particular, Norris was infuriated by the fact that the president could use lame-duck sessions in Congress to get his policies through by promising executive appointments to lame-duck Congressmen who would support him.

FAILURE BREEDS PASSION. Norris first attempted to push a constitutional amendment through Congress on December 5, 1922. Met by resistance that he attributed to an alliance between the Republican leadership in the House and the Republican-dominated executive branch, Norris failed to gain any significant support for the amendment for the next ten years. Although the Senate eventually passed the committee report on February

that improved the standard of living for America's farmers. The Rural Electrification Act (REA), which Norris sponsored, required that ownership of power generation and delivery systems be placed in the public realm, keeping them away from greedy private corporations and making electricity affordable in rural areas. The act was sharply criticized by the likes of Henry Ford and other industrialists but it won Norris the love of the rural people he represented.

In addition to the REA, Norris was a major figure in the creation of the Tennessee Valley Authority (TVA)—an engineering plan approved by Congress in 1933 to control serious flooding along the Tennessee River and its tributaries. One of the most ambitious federal engineering projects of the early twentieth century, the TVA constructed dams throughout the Tennessee River watershed, and also brought cheap electricity to this impoverished area. The REA, the TVA, and the Twentieth Amendment were seen as the highlights of Norris's service as a U.S. senator.

Norris continued to court controversy throughout his career. He was run out of the Republican party after supporting Democratic candidate Franklin Delano Roosevelt in the 1932 presidential election and won reelection in 1936 as an Independent. In 1942, however, Norris lost his bid for yet another term and he returned to his home in McCook, Nebraska, where he died in 1944. Norris was honored in 1961 by being the first person to have his bust placed in the Nebraska Hall of Fame.

13, 1923, the House let it die. The same process would happen several more times until, in January 1928, the House brought the proposal to a vote and it failed to gain the necessary two-thirds support.

Determined to prevail, Norris pushed the proposal through the Senate for a fifth time on June 7, 1929. The amendment proposal sat in the House for the next ten months before it was addressed and, again, it failed to win support. Encouraged by the fact that the Democrats had finally gained control of the House of Representatives in 1930, Norris decided to revive the amendment for a sixth time. As he had hoped, it met with much more support and, nearly ten years after Norris first addressed the issue, Congress passed the amendment and offered it to the states for ratification on March 2, 1932. Less than a year later, on

January 23, 1933, it had gained enough support to become the Twentieth Amendment to the Constitution and on February 6, 1933, it was proclaimed in effect by the secretary of state.

The amendment was nearly put to the test just nine days after it went into effect. On February 15, 1933, a deranged gunman named Giuseppe Zangara fired six shots at president-elect Franklin Delano Roosevelt as he finished addressing a crowd in Miami. The shots missed, killing Chicago Mayor Anton H. Cermak instead, but if this assassination attempt had succeeded the Twentieth Amendment would have dictated that vice president-elect John Nance Garner be inaugurated as president on March 4.

President Gerald Ford became president without being elected after the Watergate scandal. Courtesy of the Library of Congress.

Luckily the amendment was put into effect less dramatically when Roosevelt and other elected officials began their terms on the newly-set dates.

Toward a More Efficient Government

The Twentieth Amendment has proved effective in many ways. Not only has it trimmed back the transition period between presidencies and Congresses, but it has lessened the problems associated with lame duck Congressional sessions. The amendment also set the stage for the adoption of the Twenty-Fifth Amendment, which, among other things, stipulates that the vice-president-elect will become president should the president-elect die before taking office.

The Twentieth Amendment received recent attention during the impeachment proceedings against President Bill Clinton in 1998. The final House vote was taken after the 1998 elections, but the Senate was not scheduled to hear the case until after the next Congress was sworn in in 1999. Many argued, unsuccessfully, that the Twentieth Amendment required a revote by the new House. In the end, President Clinton survived the impeachment trial when the Senate acquitted him on February 12, 1999. The controversy showed that the Twentieth Amendment dramatically shortened the period within which a lame duck Congress could act, but it did not completely eliminate its ability to act.

During the impeachment proceedings against President Bill Clinton, the Twentieth Amendment received a lot of attention.

Reproduced by permission of AP/Wide World Photos.

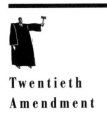

For More Information

Books

Anastaplo, George. *The Amendments to the Constitution: A Commentary.* Boston: Johns Hopkins University Press, 1995.

Bernstein, Richard B., with Jerome Agel. *Amending America: If We Love the Constitution So Much, Why Do We Keep Trying to Change It?* Lawrence: University Press of Kansas, 1995.

Grimes, Alan P. *Democracy and the Amendments to the Constitution.* New York: University Press of America, 1988.

Web Sites

Ackerman, Bruce. "Seven Stories Press: Talking Points." [Online] http://www.sevenstories.com/lametalk.htm (accessed on August 1, 2000).

"The Constitution of the United States of America." [Online] http://www.access.gpo.gov/congress/senate/constitution/amdt20.html (accessed August 1, 2000).

Nickels, Ilona. "Capitol Questions." [Online] http://www.c-span.org/questions/week165.htm (accessed August 1, 2000.)"U.S. Constitution: Twentieth Amendment." [Online] http://caselaw.findlaw.com/data/constitution/amendment20 (accessed on August 1, 2000).

"The U.S. Constitution Online." [Online] http:/www.usconstitution.net/constnot.html (accessed on August 1, 2000).

Twenty-first Amendment

SECTION 1. The eighteenth article of amendment to the Constitution of the United States is hereby repealed.

SECTION 2. The transportation or importation into any State, Territory, or possession of the United States for delivery or use therein of intoxicating liquors, in violation of the laws thereof, is hereby prohibited.

SECTION 3. The article shall be inoperative unless it shall have been ratified as an amendment to the Constitution by conventions in the several States, as provided in the Constitution, within seven years from the date of the submission hereof to the States by the Congress.

The Twenty-first Amendment is perhaps the simplest amendment to the United States Constitution. Its sole purpose is to repeal, or cancel, the earlier and very controversial Eighteenth Amendment. The Eighteenth Amendment had banned the manufacture, sale, or transport of alcoholic beverages within the United States. The Eighteenth Amendment was ratified (approved) in 1919. It came at the high point of nearly 100 years of protest against the damaging effects of alcohol consumption, and created a social experiment called "Prohibition."

The Twenty-first Amendment was ratified in 1933, and was a dramatic reversal of Prohibition. It was a real victory for those who wished to limit the federal government's power and give states the power to control local issues. In addition, the Twenty-first Amendment was the only amendment to repeal an earlier amendment. It was also the only amendment ratified by state ratifying conventions instead of state legislatures.

Temperance Advocates Push for Reform

The Eighteenth Amendment was ratified in 1919 with the best of intentions. For nearly 100 years, temperance advocates (those who believed

Twenty-first Amendment

that alcohol should be enjoyed only in moderation) had been campaigning against the dangers of alcohol consumption. They proclaimed that alcohol abuse disrupted family life, and made people unreliable workers and poor citizens.

They believed that a virtuous republic such as the United States required virtuous citizens—and there was no virtue in alcohol abuse. By the late nineteenth century, groups like the Women's Christian Temperance Union and the Anti-Saloon League had acquired enough power to convince many state and local governments to pass "dry" laws. These were laws that banned alcohol within the government's jurisdiction.

By the turn of the twentieth century, changes in the economic and social structure of the nation encouraged temperance advocates to push for broader protections against the evils of alcohol. For example, temperance advocates feared the heavy drinking habits of many newly arrived immigrants to the United States. Advocates hated the saloons and bars that thrived in the rapidly growing American cities. They argued that alcohol should be prohibited altogether.

Prohibition triumphs

Reverend Charles Stelzle's 1918 book *Why Prohibition!* helped cement Prohibition's case. In his book, Reverend Stelzle stated:

> **Drinking ... lowered industrial productivity and therefore reduced wages paid to workers; it shortened life and therefore increased the cost of insurance; it took money from other bills and therefore forced storekeepers to raise their prices in compensation; and it produced half of the business for police courts, jails, hospitals, almshouses [poorhouses], and insane asylums and therefore increased taxes to support these institutions.**

Prohibition outlawed the production, sale, and consumption of all alcoholic beverages. Reproduced by permission of the Corbis Corporation (Bellevue).

**Twenty-first
Amendment**

By 1919, the pressure for national Prohibition was so great that Congress and state legislatures ratified the Eighteenth Amendment with stunning majorities. By 1920, a year after ratification, Prohibition was the law of the land.

The perils of Prohibition

The Volstead Act of 1920 was the law that authorized the enforcement of the Eighteenth Amendment. Prohibition's backers boasted that the act would soon rid America of alcohol. For a time, it did appear that alcohol had disappeared from public life.

Eileen Lucas, author of *The Eighteenth and Twenty-First Amendments: Alcohol—Prohibition and Repeal,* quoted one man who observed that "for a year or two [Prohibition] was pretty generally observed and observed curiously enough because it did not occur to most people that it was possible to do anything else."

Journalist Ida Tarbell traveled widely across the nation as a reporter. She claimed that "One sees liquor so rarely that you forget there is such a thing." But it was not long before the popular thirst for alcohol brought drinking back into the public spotlight. This time not as a private choice, but as an illegal activity.

A NATION OF DRINKERS. Americans had always consumed alcohol. Some of the first colonists to set foot on the continent of North America brought alcohol with them. Alcohol—in the form of beer, wine, and hard liquor such as whiskey and gin—remained a popular drink through the ages.

Throughout history, the tavern or the saloon was often the gathering point in many American communities. It was a place where men could exchange news and gossip while enjoying a drink. Casual drinking was thus a regular part of many peoples' daily lives. For a time, Prohibition seemed to change these drinking habits. But it soon became clear that drinking had not been eliminated, just driven underground.

Without legal supplies, people soon found creative new ways to get their alcohol. Some turned to their doctors, many of whom were willing to write prescriptions for alcohol. Others brewed beer and wine or distilled spirits at home. The California grape industry actually enjoyed a boom when consumers learned that they could simply store grape juice for several weeks and it would turn into wine.

Perhaps most famously, Americans began to get their drinks at "speakeasies." These were places where alcohol was served illegally.

Speakeasies opened in the back rooms of restaurants, in closed saloons, or in any inconspicuous building. Entrance was often gained by a password. Once inside, patrons could enjoy drinks, music, and dancing. Many criminals made a significant profit smuggling alcohol into the country from Canada and the Caribbean Islands. Despite Prohibition, drinking continued.

A NATION OF LAWBREAKERS. Most historians agree that per capita (for each person) consumption of alcohol did drop fairly dramatically during Prohibition. However, those willing to drink illegally attracted a great deal of attention. Speakeasies became a prominent feature of most good-sized cities. The frequent raids police made on them became a staple of local news coverage. Some of the more popular magazines of the day—*Literary Digest, The New Yorker,* and *American Mercury*—celebrated the drinking that continued among the upper classes in big cities, and mocked the efforts of prohibitionists.

ILLEGAL DRINKING AND THE MOVIES. Illegal drinking was publicized quite dramatically in the movies of the day. Beginning late in the 1920s, popular films portrayed the culture of the period. The films were filled with images of wild youths dancing, drinking, and listening to jazz in hip, downtown speakeasies.

One study of films shown in 1930 was quoted in *Repealing National Prohibition.* The study found that 78 percent of films included references to liquor. It also found that 43 percent of heroes, and 23 percent of heroines, drank alcohol. Even the criminals involved in distributing illegal alcohol—the bootleggers and gangsters—were often presented as honorable characters.

Illegal liquor as a booming industry

The popularity of speakeasies soon made the illegal liquor trade a booming industry. Organized crime syndicates, or gangs of bootleggers, soon emerged to handle the complex business of obtaining, shipping, and selling alcohol. Such gangs often found that the easiest way to obtain alcohol was to steal from other bootleggers.

Gangs often engaged in open warfare with each other (see sidebar). In Chicago alone, gang warfare accounted for the deaths of 215 criminals between 1923 and 1926. Al Capone became the dominant gang leader in that violent city, and the most famous criminal of the 1920s. Gangs controlled the liquor trade in cities like Boston, Philadelphia, Detroit, Cleveland, and Denver.

FILLING A NEED: GANGSTERS

"Prohibition is a business," boasted famed bootlegger Al Capone of Chicago. "All I do is supply a public demand." In supplying the public demand for alcohol during the Prohibition years, Capone became the most famous bootlegger in the United States—and the most wanted criminal in America. But he was far from the only man making a profit from Prohibition.

No sooner had Prohibition become law in America than a number of criminals sought to make money off the distribution and sale of illegal alcohol. Along the Canadian–American border, smugglers waited for nightfall to bring shipments of illegal alcohol into the country by car, speedboat, or plane. Ships full of liquor from the Bahamas and Canada worked the coast of America. "Rum runners" darted back and forth bringing the illegal spirits to land. Once the alcohol reached shore, organized criminal gangs distributed the booze to the speakeasies that sprang up across the nation. It didn't take long to establish complex distribution networks to bring alcohol to thirsty citizens. These networks were organized and controlled by increasingly violent and dangerous criminal gangs.

Al Capone was the leader of Chicago's biggest bootlegging gang. Capone personally killed several rivals, and ordered the deaths of many

The cost of enforcement

The enforcement of Prohibition laws was handled jointly by federal, state, and local authorities. It soon proved to be more of a job than any of them could handle. Colorful Prohibition enforcement agents like Izzy Einstein and Moe Smith crafted elaborate disguises in their undercover work. But despite their notable successes, law enforcement officials found stopping the flow of illegal alcohol tremendously difficult.

Jouett Shouse oversaw Prohibition efforts for the Department of the Treasury. Shouse estimated that it would take 35,000 customs agents to stop bootleggers from smuggling alcohol into the country—he had only 6,000. During the first four years of Prohibition, the federal government alone started over 90,000 prosecutions under Prohibition laws.

others. In the mid-1920s, he led his gang on a quest to control the liquor business in Chicago. The gang war that erupted left nearly 500 gangsters dead. Eventually, Capone was tried and convicted of tax evasion—thanks in part to the efforts of FBI agent Elliott Ness, and his special unit, "The Untouchables."

Another famous bootlegger was George Remus. He was a successful lawyer who thought he could make a fortune skirting Prohibition laws. Remus found loopholes in the Volstead Act that allowed him to own both distilleries and pharmacies. He used the distilleries to make alcohol, and the pharmacies to sell liquor under government licenses. Most of the liquor Remus's companies made for the pharmacies disappeared before it reached market. Remus became rich off the illegal sale of this alcohol. He used some of his money to bribe judges and law enforcement officials. Eventually he was sent to prison, but he had made nearly $40 million dollars in a few years as one of the nation's smartest bootleggers.

Criminals and criminal gangs flourished wherever there were people who wanted to drink alcohol. However, their violence and criminal activity soon became a source of widespread social concern. Prohibition made criminals of those who merely wanted to buy a glass of beer. But it had also created a class of criminals who were more organized and more violent than any criminals the nation had ever seen. The rampant lawbreaking encouraged by Prohibition was one of the factors that led to repeal.

Twenty-first Amendment

Law enforcement agencies and prisons were soon overwhelmed. In 1929, 75,298 Prohibition cases were handled by federal courts. Many times that number were handled at the local level. The federal prison system had sheltered just 5,000 inmates in 1920. It grew to contain over 12,000 inmates ten years later—4,000 of those were imprisoned for liquor violations.

By the mid-1920s, some courts introduced a system called "bargain days." On these days, Prohibition violators could plead guilty in exchange for lighter sentences. Such sentenced included no jail time and lighter fines.

On the other hand, law enforcement officials also turned to repressive and illegal tactics to fight bootleggers. Prohibition agents sometimes

Twenty-first Amendment

The St. Valentine's Day Massacre in Chicago in 1929 was a bloody example of the violence being spurred over Prohibition. Reproduced by permission of AP/Wide World Photos.

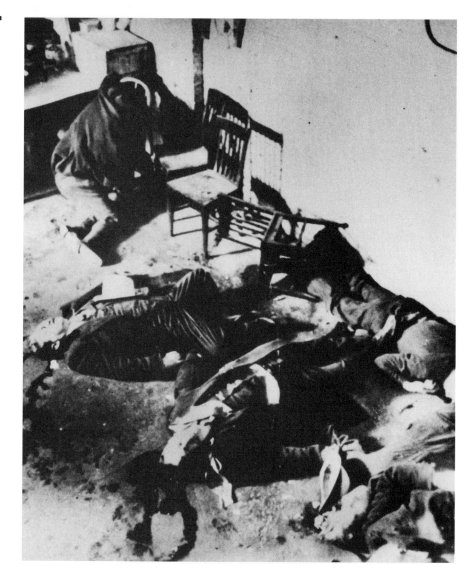

gunned down innocent citizens, stopped vehicles illegally, and even resorted to illegal wiretapping to catch criminals. In the public's eyes, it became clear that law enforcement officials simply could not keep up with the rising tide of lawlessness. And those officials might be willing to break the law themselves to gain the upper hand.

Resistance to Prohibition

By the mid-1920s, Prohibition appeared to many to be a failure. Not only were Prohibition laws unpopular, but according to David

Kyvig, they "foster[ed] criminal behavior, caus[ed] the government to take increasingly repressive enforcement action, and [bred] disrespect for all government and law." Any hopes that Prohibition would reform the American social structure were eliminated.

But repealing the Eighteenth Amendment seemed like an impossible dream. Never before had an amendment been repealed. Those opposed to the amendment feared that because ratification of a repeal amendment required a three-fourths majority, a minority of states would be able to fend off any repeal attempts. Senator Morris Sheppard had helped write the Eighteenth Amendment. He boasted, "There is as much a chance of repealing the Eighteenth Amendment as there is for a hummingbird to fly to Mars with the Washington Monument tied to its tail."

Prior to the creation of the Eighteenth Amendment, there had been little organized effort to block its passage. There were not pro-drinking groups to counter the powerful temperance and Prohibition organizations. The brewing and distilling industries lobbied against Prohibition, but they viewed each other as competitors and refused to cooperate with one other.

There was, however, a small organization called the Association Against the Prohibition Amendment (AAPA). It was formed late in 1918 by former Navy captain William H. Stayton. The association failed to create any real resistance to the Eighteenth Amendment, but its membership grew during Prohibition. By 1927, the group had reorganized, and mounted a public campaign to expose the failings of Prohibition. Along with the Voluntary Committee of Lawyers (VCL) and the Women's Organization for National Prohibition Reform (WONPR), the AAPA defined the issues that would eventually lead to the repeal of the Eighteenth Amendment (see sidebar on page 412).

The Road to Repeal

The first task of the AAPA and the VCL was to shape public opinion. They set out to do so with abandon. Both groups sent out speakers to talk to professional organizations, chambers of commerce, and other civic groups. Many of the people they spoke to were already concerned about the lawlessness of the Prohibition era.

The repeal advocates helped educate the people about the other costs associated with Prohibition. Their thoroughly researched reports argued that Americans spent a billion dollars more a year on illegal

Twenty-first Amendment

alcohol than when it was legal. Moreover, Prohibition was costing the government dearly. Reports pointed out that governments were losing hundreds of millions of dollars in excise taxes that they could have placed on alcohol. Also, they were spending staggering sums on ineffective law enforcement procedures. These reports were widely distributed and quoted in American newspapers. Kyvig estimated that the reports may have reached nearly 100 million readers.

By 1930, the tide of public opinion had also shifted away from Prohibition and toward repeal. The *Literary Digest* was a popular magazine at the time. It conducted a national opinion survey in 1922. It found that

American industrialist John D. Rockefeller, Jr. was initially pro-prohibition, but over time came to support the repeal advocates. Courtesy of the Library of Congress.

38.6 percent of Americans supported enforcing Prohibition laws, 40.8 percent wanted to modify laws to allow light wines and beer, and just 20.6 percent of people wanted to repeal Prohibition. The magazine repeated its survey in 1930. It found that 30.5 percent supported Prohibition laws (down 8 percent), 29.1 percent favored modification (down 11 percent), and 40.4 percent favored repeal (up 19.8 percent). In all, 69.5 percent of Americans supported some change in Prohibition laws.

The election of 1928

Prohibitionists, however, were not willing to give up. In 1928, Americans elected Herbert Hoover for the presidency. Hoover had called Prohibition, "a great social and economic experiment, noble in motive and far-reaching in purpose." He urged Americans to obey Prohibition laws. (The losing candidate was Democrat Alfred E. Smith. He had been the first national candidate to favor modification of the Volstead Act.)

The Congress elected in 1928 quickly passed the Jones Bill. This bill increased the fines and prison terms for those who broke liquor laws. The conservative Supreme Court made two decisions that further supported anti-liquor law enforcement: *Carroll et al v. United States* ruled that police could search automobiles suspected of containing alcohol without a warrant; and *Olmstead et al v. United States* allowed police to listen to the phone calls of people suspected of being involved in bootlegging.

The Wickersham Commission Report

Shortly after his election, President Herbert Hoover commissioned an intensive study of national Prohibition. The so-called National Commission on Law Observance and Enforcement conducted a wide-ranging study of the problems of enforcing liquor laws. The commission heard from groups both for and against Prohibition.

On January 20, 1931, Hoover released the commission's report, called the Wickersham Commission report after its chairman. Hoover issued a statement declaring that "the commission, by a large majority, does not favor the repeal of the Eighteenth Amendment as a method of cure for the inherent abuses of the liquor traffic."

It seemed that a government commission had offered its support for continuing Prohibition—until people read the report more closely. Critics pointed out that the report listed accurately all the problems with Prohibition, and seemed to indicate that existing laws were not enforceable. Despite gathering evidence that would seem to call for repeal, however, the report's conclusions came down solidly in favor of Hoover's desire to increase enforcement of Prohibition. These contradictions made many question the report's integrity. A famous editorial poem published in the *New York World* mocked the hypocrisy of the Wickersham Commission report:

> **Prohibition is an awful flop.**
> **We like it.**
> **It can't stop what it's meant to stop.**
> **We like it.**
> **It's left a trail of graft and slime,**
> **It don't prohibit worth a dime,**
> **It's filled our land with vice and crime,**
> **Nevertheless we're for it.**

Twenty-first
Amendment

THE ASSOCIATION AGAINST THE PROHIBITION AMENDMENT

By far, the most persuasive advocate for the repeal of the Eighteenth Amendment was an organization called the Association Against the Prohibition Amendment (AAPA). It was first established in 1918 by Captain William H. Stayton and several of his friends. However, the AAPA failed to achieve its first goal: stopping the passage of the Eighteenth Amendment. But the passage of Prohibition laws only confirmed the beliefs of AAPA members that the responsibility for liquor laws ought to lay with local governments. It was this core belief in the importance of local lawmaking that motivated AAPA members to fight their thirteen year battle for repeal.

The public campaign for passage of the Eighteenth Amendment had made it politically impossible to be in favor of free access to all forms of alcohol. Members of the AAPA knew that they could not appear to be in favor of a return to pre-Prohibition drinking patterns. Instead, the AAPA presented itself as an advocate for truly temperate drinking. For a time, its letterhead bore the slogan, "Beers and Light Wines NOW; But no Saloons EVER."

In the early 1920s, some of its most organized efforts went toward modifying the Volstead Act. It wanted to legalize alcoholic beverages that had an alcohol content of 2.75 percent or less. This modification was also backed by the American Federation of Labor, a large and powerful labor union. Throughout the 1920s, the AAPA's support of reasonable, temperate drinking helped it attract allies.

Encouraging temperate drinking was not the primary purpose of the AAPA, however. Stayton and other organization leaders were extremely concerned that the Eighteenth Amendment placed undue power in the hands of the federal government. The AAPA charter (a document announcing its intentions) stated that its primary objective was to educate the public about the "fundamental provisions, objects, and purposes of the Constitution of the United States ... [and] to publicly

The Depression and the politics of repeal

In the booming economic times of the 1920s, the high costs of enforcing the Prohibition laws and the decrease in tax dollars earned from taxing alcohol did not matter to most Americans. In short, when

present arguments bearing upon the necessity of keeping the powers of the several States separated from those of the Federal Government...."

In pamphlets the AAPA later published, it stated its mission more simply: "The Constitution inherited from our Fathers has been amended and mutilated.... Our Constitutional guarantees ... have been violated. The right to govern ourselves in local affairs—a right won by our ancestors in three generations of struggle—is ignored." This simple yet fundamental argument—that the Eighteenth Amendment stripped local lawmakers of the right to control local matters—formed the basis for the AAPA's push for repeal.

The AAPA's membership continued to grow throughout the early 1920s. However, internal bickering and poorly defined tactics kept the organization from gaining any ground in its fight for repeal. Late in 1927, AAPA executive James Wadsworth had Stayton's cooperation to lead a dramatic reorganization of the group. Wadsworth recruited some of America's most powerful men to serve on the AAPA's executive committee. These men included senators, House members, and wealthy industrialists.

With the political clout and financial backing of these men, the AAPA rapidly increased its efforts. The AAPA spent hundreds of thousands of dollars a year in the late 1920s and early 1930s. It financed studies showing the economic, legal, and social problems caused by Prohibition. It pushed for changes to liquor laws on a national and local basis. It lobbied politicians to support repeal. Throughout this period, public support for repeal grew steadily—thanks in large part to the efforts of the now well-organized and powerful AAPA.

By 1928, the AAPA began to exert real influence on the Democratic party, but they were unable to place a call for repeal on the presidential party platform. By 1932, however, it was a different story. Along with other anti-Prohibition groups, the AAPA had convinced the Democratic Party to support repeal of the Eighteenth Amendment. Soon after Franklin Delano Roosevelt's election, they achieved their long-sought goal with the passage of the Twenty-first Amendment.

times were good, America could afford to fund Prohibition. But the stock market collapse of 1929, and the worldwide economic depression that followed, soon made the costs of enforcing Prohibition an expendable luxury.

**Twenty-first
Amendment**

According to Eileen Lucas, anti-Prohibitionists "argued that repeal of prohibition would increase government revenue, reduce taxes, create jobs, and expand markets for farm goods." Labor leaders claimed that allowing beer production alone would create 250,000 jobs. Lucas added, "Humorist Will Rogers was not being funny when he pointed out, 'What does Prohibition amount to if your neighbor's children are not eating? It's food, not drink, that is our problem now.'"

By the Presidential election of 1932, repeal had become a serious campaign issue. Hoover and the Republicans continued their support of Prohibition. However, there was an extended debate in the Democratic Party. Finally, they came to agreement. And their candidate, Franklin Delano Roosevelt, came down solidly on the side of repeal. When accepting his party's nomination, Roosevelt proclaimed, "This convention wants repeal. Your candidate wants repeal. And I am confident that the United States wants repeal. From this date on, the Eighteenth Amendment is doomed!"

The beginning of the end

On November 8, 1932, Roosevelt—known popularly as FDR—won a decisive victory in the presidential election. Equally important to backers of repeal, anti-Prohibitionists, or wets as they were called, gained substantial strength in Congress. According to Kyvig, "the *New York Times* calculated that the Seventy-third Congress would have 343 wet Representatives and 61 wet Senators." Most of these politicians took the election results as a mandate (order) for repeal. A *Literary Digest* public opinion poll seconded public support for repeal. Offered a simple choice between continuing support for the Eighteenth Amendment and repeal, 73.5 percent of Americans supported repeal.

NO TIME TO WASTE. Following the election of 1932, the pace of action toward repeal quickened considerably. Repeal advocates did not want to wait for the new Congress to convene to vote on repeal. They proposed a repeal amendment to the sitting Congress on December 5, 1932. They came up just six votes short of the two-thirds majority needed for passage.

The Senate began its debate of a repeal resolution in February 1933. Senator Morris Sheppard attempted a filibuster (a lengthy speech intended to obstruct the passage of legislation) to avoid a vote. But the Senate voted to send the Twenty-first Amendment to the states by a count of 63 to 23. On February 20, the House seconded the repeal amendment by a vote of 289 to 121.

Roosevelt acted just as quickly. Shortly after taking office on March 4, 1933, he cut funding for the federal Prohibition Bureau. He also asked Congress to modify the Volstead Act to allow the sale of beer. This latter legislation was signed into law by FDR on April 7th.

The few breweries that had stayed in business through Prohibition quit removing the alcohol from their beer. They began shipping "real" beer just after midnight on April 7, 1933. Beer lovers in the brewing center of Milwaukee, Wisconsin, celebrated the day as if it was a holiday. A plane took off for Washington, D.C., to deliver President Roosevelt his first shipment of beer. Congress and the president had now signaled their desire to bring Prohibition to an end. But it was up to the states to make repeal the law of the land. They would do so by novel means.

STATE CONVENTIONS. Prior to the Twenty-first Amendment, every constitutional amendment had been approved by state legislatures. But Article V of the Constitution also authorized Congress to present proposed amendments to "conventions." Congress chose to send the Twenty-first Amendment to state conventions because they felt state conventions would better represent the will of the people. Also, it would not allow the minority of dry states to hold repeal hostage. The only problem was that no one knew exactly how state conventions should be formed.

The Voluntary Committee of Lawyers (VCL) had long supported repeal. Luckily, it stepped in to draft and propose model legislation that would provide for the creation of state conventions. Instead of allowing already-seated state legislators to cast votes, the legislation called for the election of convention delegates. The delegates would be appointed in proportion to the popular vote. Many states adopted the VCL's legislation as it was written, and others adopted it to meet their needs.

On April 10, 1933, Michigan became the first state to vote for repeal of the Eighteenth Amendment. Many expected resistance from strong dry states like Indiana, Texas, and Maine. However, each of these states also quickly voted for repeal. On December 5, 1933, Utah became the thirty-sixth—and decisive—state to cast its vote for the Twenty-first Amendment. With Utah's vote, national Prohibition was over. For the first time in history, a Constitutional amendment had been repealed.

America After Repeal

Contrary to the fears of temperance advocates, the end of Prohibition did not bring about a rash of alcohol-related social problems. In fact, all the

Twenty-first
Amendment

Twenty-first Amendment

The repeal of the Eighteenth Amendment was met with great celebration. Reproduced by permission of AP/Wide World Photos.

benefits that repeal advocates had promised were quickly realized. Americans were now more temperate. Per capita consumption of alcohol after the repeal of Prohibition only reached 60 percent of what it had been in the years before Prohibition. This indicated that many Americans had stopped abusing alcohol to the degree that they once had. In fact, the biggest celebrations occurred around the reintroduction of beer in April 1933, and not around the final passage of the Twenty-first Amendment.

Widespread disregard for the law declined dramatically. After all, the law now suited the majority of the people. Perhaps most importantly, repeal brought real economic benefits to Americans who were enduring a lasting depression. According to an industry survey cited by David Kyvig, by 1940 "the manufacture and sale of alcoholic beverages generated ... 1,229,000 jobs and a billion dollars in wages. Federal, state, and local tax and license receipts amounted to another one billion dollars."

Liquor legislation lives on

The repeal of Prohibition did not mean the end of liquor legislation. Instead, it meant that alcohol use would now be regulated at the local and state level. This is exactly where many repeal advocates felt such control

should exist. Many states chose to license and regulate the private sale of alcohol. Others allowed the sale of alcoholic beverages only in state-run liquor stores. Others chose a combination of these methods.

Most states now regulate the location of establishments selling alcohol (not allowing them near schools or churches, for example). States also determine the age at which people can purchase alcohol (the age is now twenty-one in every state), and regulate alcohol advertising. While alcohol is now available in most parts of the country, some communities have preferred to remain dry even into the twenty-first century.

The nature of alcohol consumption was certainly changed by Prohibition. Temperance advocates viewed saloons as centers of sin, but they largely disappeared from the American social scene thanks to local liquor laws. The laws banned selling liquor by the drink, prevented the sale of liquor to intoxicated people, or insisted that alcohol only be served with food. Many of these laws have been made less strict over time, but they did serve to end forever the saloon as a forum for public drunkenness.

The packaging of liquor also changed as a result of Prohibition. During Prohibition, soft drink bottlers learned how to package drinks in single-serving cans or bottles. Consumers found that they could store these beverages in another new device, the refrigerator. With repeal, more and more Americans were able to buy small amounts of alcohol, and store it in the home for later consumption. The home, rather than the saloon, became the center for alcohol consumption. Temperance advocates were happy for this change. They felt that alcohol abuse would occur less in the home.

The Constitution After Repeal

The Twenty-first Amendment was important because it ended the great social experiment: Prohibition. But as the first amendment to undo an earlier constitutional amendment, it also held important lessons about the meaning and uses of constitutional amendments in general.

Five amendments were rapidly passed between 1909 and 1932. Some Americans were encouraged to think of constitutional amendments as a powerful tool for shaping the government to suit their needs. Such thinking had led to amendments allowing women to vote, and allowing for the direct election of senators. But the Eighteenth Amendment had clearly overstepped the bounds of what was acceptable when it tried to limit individual actions in the name of morality. The result was the creation of laws that were very unpopular, and were widely disregarded.

The repeal of the Eighteenth Amendment clearly indicated that there was a limit to what could be accomplished through constitutional amendments. The passage of the Twenty-first Amendment helped lawmakers see that they could not create laws that ran counter to popular opinion. It convinced many lawmakers that some powers were better left to state and local governments, or to personal choice. "After Prohibition," wrote Kyvig, "American lawmakers became cautious about launching another major attempt to reshape individual behavior."

The Future of Alcohol in America

Sadly, neither the Eighteenth nor Twenty-first Amendments solved the problem of alcohol in America. "According to the National Council on Alcoholism," writes Lucas, "alcohol is a contributing factor in more than fifteen thousand deaths and 6 million injuries due to accidents each year. It is also a leading cause of crime."

Underage drinking (drinking by those beneath the legal drinking age) is also a leading cause of crime and traffic accidents. The American experience with Prohibition probably means that Prohibition will never again be attempted on a national scale. However, legislators continue to struggle to craft laws and policies that help America encourage temperate drinking.

For More Information

Books

Barry, James P. *The Noble Experiment, 1919–1933: The Eighteenth Amendment Prohibits Liquor in America.* New York: Franklin Watts, 1972.

Behr, Edward. *Prohibition: Thirteen Years that Changed America.* New York: Arcade Publishing, 1996.

Bernstein, Richard B., with Jerome Agel. *Amending America: If We Love the Constitution So Much, Why Do We Keep Trying to Change It?* New York: Times Books/Random House, 1993; Lawrence, KS: University Press of Kansas, 1995.

Cohen, Daniel. *Prohibition: America Makes Alcohol Illegal.* Brookfield, CT: Millbrook Press, 1995.

Hintz, Martin. *Farewell, John Barleycorn: Prohibition in the United States*. Minneapolis, MN: Lerner Publications, 1996.

Kobler, John. *Ardent Spirits: The Rise and Fall of Prohibition*. New York: G. P. Putnam's Sons, 1973.

Kyvig, David E., editor. *Law, Alcohol, and Order: Perspectives on National Prohibition*. Westport, CT: Greenwood Press, 1985.

Kyvig, David E. *Repealing National Prohibition*. Chicago, IL: The University of Chicago Press, 1979.

Lucas, Eileen. *The Eighteenth and Twenty-First Amendments: Alcohol— Prohibition and Repeal*. Springfield, NJ: Enslow Publishers, 1998.

Rebman, Renee C. *Prohibition*. San Diego, CA: Lucent Books, 1998.

Rumbarger, John J. *Profits, Power, and Prohibition: Alcohol Reform and the Industrializing of America, 1800–1930*. Albany, NY: State University of New York Press, 1989.

Sann, Paul. *The Lawless Decade*. New York: Crown, 1957.

Taylor, Robert Lewis. *Vessel of Wrath: The Life and Times of Carry Nation*. New York: New American Library, 1966.

Web sites

Kyvig, David. "Repealing National Prohibition." [Online] http://www.druglibrary.org/schaffer/history/rnp/rnptoc.htm. (accessed August 3, 2000).

McWilliams, Peter. "Prohibition: A Lesson in the Futility (and Danger) of Prohibiting." [Online] http://www.mcwilliams.com/books/aint/402.htm. (accessed August 3, 2000).

"Temperance and Prohibition." [Online] http://www.history.ohio-state.edu/projects/prohibition/contents.htm. (accessed August 2, 2000).

Twenty-second Amendment

SECTION 1. No person shall be elected to the office of the President more than twice, and no person who has held the office of President, or acted as President, for more than two years of a term to which some other person was elected President shall be elected to the office of the President more than once. But this Article shall not apply to any person holding the office of President when this article was proposed by the Congress, and shall not prevent any person who may be holding the office of President, or acting as President, during the term within which this Article becomes operative from holding the office of President or acting as President during the remainder of such term.

SECTION 2. This article shall be inoperative unless it shall have been ratified as an amendment to the Constitution by the legislatures of three-fourths of the several States within seven years from the date of its submission to the States by the Congress.

Few amendments have been passed with as little popular attention as the Twenty-second Amendment. The amendment limits a president to two terms in office. To its backers, it gave a two-term tradition constitutional status. The two-term tradition had dominated the American presidency—until the time that President Franklin Delano Roosevelt (FDR) was elected for a third term in 1940 (and to a fourth in 1944). To its critics, the amendment was a politically-motivated insult to the memory of FDR. (He had been one of the most popular presidents of the twentieth century.) Debates about the amendment's necessity continued for years after its passage. Calls for its repeal continue to the present day.

Limiting the Executive's Power

The authors of the Constitution faced many major problems. Among them, the need for an executive officer strong enough to lead, but not so strong that

RATIFICATION FACTS

PROPOSED: Submitted by Congress to the states on March 21, 1947.

RATIFICATION: Ratified by the required three-fourths of states (thirty-six of forty-eight) on February 27, 1951, and by five more states on May 4, 1951. Declared to be part of the Constitution on March 1, 1951.

RATIFYING STATES: Maine, March 31, 1947; Michigan, March 31, 1947; Iowa, April 1, 1947; Kansas, April 1, 1947; New Hampshire, April 1, 1947; Delaware, April 2, 1947; Illinois, April 3, 1947; Oregon, April 3, 1947; Colorado, April 12, 1947; California, April 15, 1947; New Jersey, April 15, 1947; Vermont, April 15, 1947; Ohio, April 16, 1947; Wisconsin, April 16, 1947; Pennsylvania, April 29, 1947; Connecticut, May 21, 1947; Missouri, May 22, 1947; Nebraska, May 23, 1947; Virginia, January 28, 1948; Mississippi, February 12, 1948; New York, March 9, 1948; South Dakota, January 21, 1949; North Dakota, February 25, 1949; Louisiana, May 17, 1950; Montana, January 25, 1951; Indiana, January 29, 1951; Idaho, January 30, 1951; New Mexico, February 12, 1951; Wyoming, February 12, 1951; Arkansas, February 15, 1951; Georgia, February 17, 1951; Tennessee, February 20, 1951; Texas, February 22, 1951; Nevada, February 26, 1951; Utah, February 26, 1951; Minnesota, February 27, 1951.

he would dominate the other branches of government. They surveyed the executive officers of other countries, especially Great Britain. They mostly wanted to avoid allowing the executive to remain in power for too long. They believed presidents or kings who remained in power too long quit caring about the people's concerns, and only worked to preserve their power. The last thing the Americans wanted was to create another monarchy.

The Americans who wrote the Constitution in 1787 had good reason to fear giving chief executives too much power. They had revolted against England because they believed that King George III ignored the needs of his subjects in the American colonies. And also because of their hatred of colonial governors. Many colonial governors held office for extended periods, and used their office for personal gain.

After the American Revolution (1775–1783), some state constitution writers did away with the office of governor. Others severely limited the number of years and terms that a governor could serve. Such constitutions supported the principle of "rotation in office." This meant that public servants would hold their offices for a short time, and would be replaced with newly elected people. The idea behind this was to make elected officials behave more responsibly—especially since they knew that they had to live as citizens under the laws and policies they created while in office.

The Second Continental Congress created the Articles of Confederation to provide a federal government for the newly independent colonies. But it did not create a separate executive office, or presidency. Instead, it allowed Congress to elect its own president to serve a single one-year term in office. But this was a weakness, and one of the many problems that led Americans to replace the Articles of Confederation with the Constitution. The Constitution created separate executive, legislative, and judicial branches. But now the Constitution's framers (the people who wrote the Constitution) faced a new problem: how best to establish the office of the president.

Establishing the Two-term Tradition

The Federal Convention met in Philadelphia in May of 1787 to write the Constitution. "The Framers," wrote constitutional scholar Richard B. Bernstein, "concluded that repeated eligibility for a short term of office would balance the two goals they sought in designing the Presidency—a President powerful enough to administer the government and secure national objectives, yet limited enough that he would not become a tyrant or a monarch."

After much argument and compromise, the delegates to the convention settled upon an agreement. The chief executive would serve a four-year term, and would seek reelection as often as he wanted. The delegates rested secure, because the first president was a man with a reputation for passing on the reins of power once he had served his term. This man was George Washington.

Washington was unanimously elected to the presidency in 1788. His immense personal prestige helped him guide the fledgling government to a stable beginning. Washington was a calming figure. He helped moderate the frequent clashes between Federalists and Republicans (two early political parties with very different ideas about how the country ought to be run).

Alexander Hamilton and Thomas Jefferson were the leaders of the Federalists and the Republicans respectively. Hamilton and Jefferson tried to convince the reluctant Washington to run for another term. But in 1796, Washington an-nounced that he would retire at the end of his second term. His retirement, and the successful transfer of power to a new president, set a precedent that lasted for nearly 150 years.

The two-term tradition in action

Thomas Jefferson was a delegate to the first constitutional convention. He had been a strong supporter of limiting the presidency to a single term in office. (He originally preferred a single seven-year

George Washington set the precedent of retiring from the presidency after two terms. Courtesy of the Library of Congress.

term.) He changed his mind after he became the nation's third president in 1800, and decided to seek reelection in 1804. Jefferson explained his thinking as quoted in Kris Palmer's *Constitutional Amendments:*

> **General Washington set the example of voluntary retirement after eight years. I shall follow it, and a few more precedents will oppose the obstacle of habit to any one after a while who shall endeavor to extend his term. Perhaps it may beget a disposition to establish it by an amendment of the Constitution**

With these words, Jefferson became the first to announce the two-term tradition. He was neither the first, nor the last, to suggest that the tradition be written into law through a constitutional amendment.

Twenty-second Amendment

TEDDY ROOSEVELT: CHALLENGING THE TWO-TERM TRADITION

Franklin Delano Roosevelt was the first American president to break the two-term tradition. Years before, however, his cousin, Theodore Roosevelt, severely tested the limits of this political tradition. Teddy Roosevelt was elected vice president to President William McKinley in the election of 1900. McKinley was assassinated in 1901. This placed the forty-three-year-old Roosevelt in the White House with three years left in his term.

He was reelected to the presidency in 1904, and began his second term in office—or was it his first? Since he had succeeded McKinley in office, some argued that Roosevelt's election victory in 1904 was the start of his first term. Thus, he could be elected again in 1908.

Teddy Roosevelt himself stopped such speculation. After his victory in 1904, he declared that he had already served for three and a half years of McKinley's term, and his next term would be his last. "The wise custom which limits the President to two terms regards the substance and not the form," stated Roosevelt, "and under no circumstances will I be a candidate for or accept another nomination." These words would come back to haunt him.

Challenges to the two-term tradition

Throughout the nineteenth century, presidents remained true to the two-term tradition. Presidents James Madison, James Monroe, and Andrew Jackson all resigned willingly at the end of their second term. Other presidents were either defeated for reelection or, as in the case of Abraham Lincoln, were assassinated during their second term. It was not until the Ulysses S. Grant administration that any president even considered running for a third term.

FLIRTING WITH A THIRD TERM. General Grant had earned the nation's admiration for his leadership during the Civil War (1861–1865). He was elected president in 1868, and tried to help the nation heal its wounds from the recently concluded war. His second term was plagued by scandals, but his Republican party could not find any candidate they liked as well as Grant. Supporters promoted the idea that Grant should run for a

Roosevelt was the youngest man ever to hold the presidency. He often regretted his words concerning reelection, but he stuck to them for the 1908 election. Roosevelt backed William Howard Taft of Ohio for the presidency, and was pleased when Taft won. But that pleasure soon soured as Roosevelt came to believe that the Taft administration was not living up to the policies he had begun. In 1912, Roosevelt announced that he would run against Taft for the Republican presidential nomination. Conservatives within the party blocked Roosevelt's nomination, however, and Roosevelt left the party.

Convinced of his political policies and his popular support, Roosevelt formed a new party, the Progressive Party. He accepted its nomination for the presidency. He became the first presidential candidate to seek what most Americans believed was a third term. Roosevelt reversed the position he had taken in his 1904 statement. He declared that this would only be his second term. Most Americans believed he was right the first time. One popular anti-Roosevelt campaign button read "WASHINGTON WOULDN'T, GRANT COULDN'T, ROOSEVELT SHOULDN'T." In the end, the voters agreed and elected Democrat Woodrow Wilson as President. It would take another Roosevelt— Franklin Delano—to finally break the two-term tradition.

third term in 1876. The idea was emphatically rejected by the public, and by Congress. It passed a resolution that declared that breaking the two-term tradition would be "unwise, unpatriotic, and fraught with peril to our free institutions."

Under slightly different circumstances twenty years later, President Grover Cleveland attempted to secure a third term. Like Grant, he met with resistance. Cleveland had served his first term from 1884 to 1888. He then lost his bid for reelection. He regained the presidency in 1892. In 1896, he sought to secure the Democratic party nomination for what would have been his third term.

Again, however, widespread resistance to breaking the two-term tradition kept Cleveland from even securing the nomination. Instead, the Democratic party nominated William Jennings Bryan. He lost the election to Republican William McKinley. Cleveland's supporters considered nominating him again in 1904, but Cleveland wisely refused.

**Twenty-second
Amendment**

The two-term tradition in the twentieth century

The twentieth century saw several significant challenges to the two-term tradition. When Theodore Roosevelt campaigned for the presidency in 1912, he argued that his first administration should not count toward his two terms. He had served as president upon the assassination of President William McKinley in 1900, and did not count this term as his own. He was convinced that he had not had enough time to enact the programs and policies he was elected to enact. Roosevelt won the Progressive Party nomination, but lost the election to Woodrow Wilson (see sidebar on page 424).

Woodrow Wilson also flirted with the idea of seeking the presidency for a third term. Wilson was a noted political scientist and historian. He had once criticized the tradition that drove presidents from office just as they had mastered this most complex and challenging of jobs. Wilson was committed to his foreign policy objectives—especially the creation of a League of Nations (a precursor to the United Nations). Towards the end of his second term, he thought seriously of seeking re-nomination in 1920. In the end, however, Wilson's declining health and the Democratic Party leaders' fear of breaking with tradition led to the nomination of James M. Cox. He lost to Warren G. Harding.

COOLIDGE'S CURIOUS INTENTIONS. Like Theodore Roosevelt had done when McKinley died, Vice President Calvin Coolidge took over the presidency when President Warren Harding died midway through his term in 1923. Coolidge served the remaining nineteen months of Harding's term, and then won a term of his own. The question was, once again, could he be elected for yet another term in office? Supporters—and Coolidge had many—argued that since he had served less than half of Harding's term, he should be able to run again. Many political analysts agreed that the two-term tradition was out of date, and also thought Coolidge should end the tradition.

Coolidge himself remained neutral on the idea of a third term until August 2, 1927, when he delivered a brief, handwritten message to the press: "I do not choose to run for President in nineteen twenty-eight." The news flashed around the nation, but it did not altogether stop speculation that Coolidge would in fact try for a third time. Rumors spread that the message was, in fact, a subtle attempt to get his party to draft him for a nomination he felt he could not pursue openly.

The House of Representatives issued a resolution urging him against a third term. Coolidge refrained from running. Historians continue to speculate whether Coolidge really meant to retire or not. Their speculations were fueled by the memoirs of a minor White House employee. The employee insisted that Coolidge truly hoped that he would be nominated once more.

FDR breaks the tradition

In 1932, Franklin Delano Roosevelt (popularly known as FDR) won election as president of the United States. Eight years later, he had led America through, and nearly out of, the worst economic depression in the country's history. With no clear successor, and with Europe gripped by a struggle that would soon be known as World War II, Roosevelt broke with tradition. He was determined to seek reelection for a third time.

Roosevelt spoke on the campaign trail about the war in Europe. As quoted in David E. Kyvig's *Explicit and Authentic Acts: Amending the U.S. Constitution, 1776-1995,* Roosevelt said: "There is a great storm raging now, a storm that makes things harder for the world. And that storm, which did not start in this land of ours, is the true reason that I would like to stick by these people of ours until we reach the clear, sure footing ahead."

Franklin Roosevelt (center) was elected to the office of president four times. Courtesy of the Library of Congress.

*Eleanor Roosevelt
preferred that her
husband not seek a
third term.* Reproduced
by permission of AP/Wide
World Photos.

Republican opponents were furious at FDR's break with convention. Several state legislatures adopted anti-third-term resolutions. According to Kyvig, the Republican national convention "pledged to seek a constitutional two-term limit 'to insure against the overthrow of our American system of government,' and their nominee Wendell Wilkie declared that, if elected, such a measure would be his first request of Congress." Despite these objections, Roosevelt won. But by a much smaller margin than he had enjoyed in his first two presidential victories.

But Roosevelt's presidency did not stop at a third term. The country was still embroiled (heavily involved) in World War II during the 1944 presidential election. Roosevelt was once again elected president. Republicans across the country howled with anger. More states passed resolutions demanding term limits, and fifteen members of the U.S. Congress introduced term-limit amendments. Roosevelt's defenders insisted that the need to maintain consistent policies during wartime justified his extended service, but such arguments did not convince the opposition.

Roosevelt did not live to see the end of the war. He died on April 12, 1945. This left Vice President Harry Truman to serve out his term, and lead the nation to victory in World War II.

A Republican Amendment

In 1946, with the war over and an unpopular Truman in office, Republicans swept to victory in Congressional elections. Republican leaders vowed that they would take steps to make sure that no president ever served a third term again.

January 3, 1947, was the first day of the Congressional session. House member Earl C. Michener of Michigan introduced an amendment resolution calling for term limits on the presidency. After a brief period of debate on February 6, 1947, every House Republican as well as many Southern Democrats voted for the term limit amendment by a count of 285 to 121.

House Republican Karl Mundt was quoted in *Explicit and Authentic Acts*. He expressed the opinions of many when he said that the amendment "grows directly out of the unfortunate experience we had in this country in 1940 and again in 1944 when a President who had entrenched [established] himself in power by use of patronage and the public purse refused to vacate the office at the conclusion of two terms, but used the great powers of the Presidency to perpetuate himself in office."

Democrats oppose the proposed amendment

Most Democrats opposed term limits on the same principles that had kept term limits from being part of the original Constitution. Democrats insisted that the people should have the power to elect whoever they wanted for as long as they wanted. They borrowed Alexander Hamilton's argument. Term limits would deprive the people of the most experienced

Twenty-second Amendment

Near the end of the presidency of popular president Dwight D. Eisenhower, the Republicans started to wonder if the Twenty-second Amendment had been a mistake.

chief executive, and would limit the people's right to stick with a candidate in a time of crisis, such as the war that had just ended.

But Republican support was too strong. The Senate did change the amendment, however. The change permitted someone elevated to the presidency due to the death or removal of a sitting president to be elected twice to their own presidential candidacies. The amendment passed by a vote of 59 to 23 on March 12, 1947. (The amendment also said that the amendment would not affect Truman, the sitting president.) Democrats complained that the amendment was merely an attempt to dishonor the memory of a Democratic president, but the House sent the amendment to the states for ratification on March 21, 1947.

RATIFICATION. The Twenty-second Amendment was immensely popular among Republicans. It was quickly ratified by most of the states with Republican-controlled legislatures. Northern Democratic states followed their party's position and largely rejected the bill. Most Democratic legislatures in Southern states, however, rejected the party line and approved the amendment. On February 27, 1951, the Twenty-second Amendment became law.

Many speculated as to whether the Twenty-second Amendment might be repealed for another popular president: Ronald Reagan. Courtesy of the Library of Congress.

According to Kyvig, one liberal journal had observed that the amendment "glided through legislatures in a fog of silence—passed by men whose election in no way involved their stand on the question—without hearings, without publicity, without any of that popular participation that should have accompanied a change in the organic law of the country."

A Workable Amendment?

The Twenty-second Amendment passed under strange conditions. The amendment was largely ignored by the public, and had taken longer to ratify than any other amendment in the history of the Constitution to date. Not long after the amendment was ratified, its most ardent backers—the Republican party—wondered if their amendment had been a mistake. Popular Republican President Dwight D. Eisenhower was nearing the end of his second term. His party dearly wished that he could take a third term. They even considered mounting a campaign for repeal of the amendment.

Repeal

Two more times in the following years, Republican presidents won second terms. This sparked further calls for repeal of the term limit amendment. Richard Nixon's reelection in 1972, and Ronald Reagan's reelection in 1984, allowed the Republican party to dream of a political

TERM LIMITS FOR CONGRESS

The Twenty-second Amendment placed limits on the number of terms a president may serve. Some began calling for term limits for members of Congress as well. During the early years of American history, few legislators served more than a few terms in office, and Congress truly was run by citizens. But by the late twentieth century, many senators and representatives had, in the words of constitutional scholar Richard B. Bernstein, "racked up careers of two, three, or even four decades of service." Simply, they had become career politicians.

Career politicians worried critics, and many no longer listened to their constituents. They happily enjoyed the perks of their office: the status, the office staff, the influence. In 1991, a banking scandal revealed that many House members had been abusing the banking privileges they enjoyed at the House credit union. They wrote checks for more money than they had in their account. This banking scandal brought intense public attention to long-serving Congressmen.

Alan Ehrenhalt, author of *The United States of Ambition: Politicians, Power, and the Pursuit of Office,* writes:

> [O]fficeholders comprise a career elite whose lifetime political preoccupation has separated them from most people.... There is something about the image of the entrenched con-

dynasty should they gain repeal. But in both cases other circumstances helped crush the movement for a third term.

Nixon's dynasty was brought down by the Watergate scandal. This scandal drove him to resign in 1974. Ronald Reagan's advancing years and declining memory made it wise for him to leave office in 1989 at the age of 78. Democratic President Bill Clinton remained popular at the end of his second term, but his own scandal-ridden presidency had sparked no calls for a third term. But an amendment to repeal presidential term limits was once again offered in 1999.

There have been real efforts to secure repeal over the years. Republican House representative Guy Vander Jagt tried to introduce a repeal amendment in Congress between 1972 and 1991, but the amendment gained little support. Some scholars and politicians continued to support

gressional incumbent, immersed in politics as his life's work and impregnable [unshakable] in an elected office that pays $125,000 a year, that challenges some fundamental American notions of democracy and fairness.

Many Americans agreed.

In 1994, Republican candidates for Congress rallied behind a set of proposals for reform that they called the "Contract with America." Among their promises was one to secure a constitutional amendment to limit the terms of members of Congress. Though the House voted on several proposals, none received a two-thirds majority. Proposals before the Senate never came up for a vote. The main problem was the House members could not agree on exactly how to limit service. Some proposed that the limit be six years, while others backed a twelve-year limit.

If nothing else, the defeat of term limits in Congress revealed that there were very good reasons to allow voters the opportunity to reelect their representatives as often as they wished. Despite the dangers associated with career politicians, most voters recognized that experienced politicians were often best suited to protect the interests of the people, because they had mastered the difficulties of getting what they wanted. In the end, most believed that the best way to limit a Congressional term was at the ballot box.

the idea. They adopted all the same arguments that had kept term limits out of the Constitution for so many years. Repeal advocates argued that voters should be able to choose who they want. Other reformers have called for a single six-year term for the presidency. This proposal has been offered to Congress 160 times over the course of two centuries, and has earned the support of fifteen Presidents.

Is the Twenty-second Amendment Here to Stay?

In the end, however, the Twenty-second Amendment has earned much respect and support. In the 1990s, many Americans became distrustful of politicians who spent many years in office. Term limits for other elected officials became increasingly popular (see sidebar on page 432).

According to Bernstein, even the amendment's critics have come to see that it may help to guarantee Americans the best possible presidency. Bernstein noted that the modern presidency exerts such a toll on the president's health that it would be difficult for any man to withstand a third term. Moreover, the second term of most presidents has been far less successful than the first. This makes it unlikely that a president would be strong enough politically to manage a third term.

Perhaps the strongest argument for the Twenty-second Amendment is history. For over 150 years, the two-term tradition successfully guided the peaceful transition of power, and ensured that no one president ever gained too much power. As Thomas Jefferson had wished, that two-term tradition is now part of the Constitution.

For More Information

Bernstein, Richard B., with Jerome Agel. *Amending America: If We Love the Constitution So Much, Why Do We Keep Trying to Change It?* New York: Times Books, 1993.

Carey, John M. *Term Limits and Legislative Representation.* New York: Cambridge University Press, 1996.

Ehrenhalt, Alan. *The United States of Ambition: Politicians, Power, and the Pursuit of Office.* New York: Times Books, 1991; revised, 1992.

Feinberg, Barbara S. *The Amendments.* New York: Henry Holt, 1996.

Flynn, Vance. *Term Limits.* New York: Pocket Books, 1997.

Katz, William Loren, and Bernard Gaughran. *The Constitutional Amendments.* New York: Watts, 1974.

Kyvig, David E. *Explicit and Authentic Acts: Amending the U.S. Constitution, 1776–1995.* Lawrence, KS: University of Press of Kansas, 1996.

Morin, Isobel V. *Our Changing Constitution: How and Why We Have Amended It.* Brookfield, CT: Millbrook Press, 1998.

Palmer, Kris E., editor. *Constitutional Amendments, 1789 to the Present.* Detroit, MI: Gale Group, 2000.

Racheter, Donald P., Richard E. Wagner, and Holbert L. Harris, editors. *Limiting Leviathan.* Northampton, MA: Edward Elgar Publishing, 1999.

Will, George F. *Restoration.* New York: The Free Press, 1993.

Twenty-third Amendment

SECTION 1. The District constituting the seat of Government of the United States shall appoint in such manner as the Congress may direct:

A number of electors of President and Vice President equal to the whole number of Senators and Representatives in Congress to which the District would be entitled if it were a State, but in no event more than the least populous State; they shall be in addition to those appointed by the States, but they shall be considered, for the purposes of the election of President and Vice President, to be electors appointed by a State; and they shall meet in the District and perform such duties as provided by the twelfth article of amendment.

SECTION 2. The Congress shall have power to enforce this article by appropriate legislation.

The Twenty-third Amendment provides the citizens of the District of Columbia the right to vote in national elections for president and vice president of the United States. In large part, the amendment was crafted in response to the unexpected growth of Washington, D.C., the home of the federal government. The District of Columbia is commonly referred to by residents as "the nation's last colony" because it is not a state. (It had a population of more than 600,000 people in the 1990 census.) The amendment addressed a problem with the political status of the capital that had existed since its creation.

The residents of the District of Columbia have always had a strange status in American politics. They have all the obligations of citizenship—such as payment of federal and local taxes, and service in the armed forces—but for years they did not enjoy the most basic privilege of voting in national elections. The Twenty-third Amendment addressed this contradiction. Unfortunately, it did not answer concerns about the

RATIFICATION FACTS

PROPOSED: Submitted by Congress to the states on June 16, 1960.

RATIFICATION: Ratified by the required three-fourths of states (thirty-eight of fifty) on March 29, 1961, and by one more state on March 30, 1961. Declared to be part of the Constitution on April 3, 1961.

RATIFYING STATES: Hawaii, June 23, 1960 (Hawaii made a technical correction to its resolution on June 30, 1960); Massachusetts, August 22, 1960; New Jersey, December 19, 1960; New York, January 17, 1961; California, January 19, 1961; Oregon, January 27, 1961; Maryland, January 30, 1961; Idaho, January 31, 1961; Maine, January 31, 1961; Minnesota, January 31, 1961; New Mexico, February 1, 1961; Nevada, February 2, 1961; Montana, February 6, 1961; South Dakota, February 6, 1961; Colorado, February 8, 1961; Washington, February 9, 1961; West Virginia, February 9, 1961; Alaska, February 10, 1961; Wyoming, February 13, 1961; Delaware, February 20, 1961; Utah, February 21, 1961; Wisconsin, February 21, 1961; Pennsylvania, February 28, 1961; Indiana, March 3, 1961; North Dakota, March 3, 1961; Tennessee, March 6, 1961; Michigan, March 8, 1961; Connecticut, March 9, 1961; Arizona, March 10, 1961; Illinois, March 14, 1961; Nebraska, March 15, 1961; Vermont, March 15, 1961; Iowa, March 16, 1961; Missouri, March 20, 1961; Oklahoma, March 21, 1961; Rhode Island, March 22, 1961; Kansas, March 29, 1961; Ohio, March 29, 1961.

district's lack of Congressional representation, or local control of district affairs. An unratified amendment concerning such issues failed to gain approval from the states in the mid-1980s. The Twenty-third Amendment is the only amendment that alters the electoral process outlined in the Constitution and modified by the Twelfth Amendment.

The Need for a National Capital

The political status of the District of Columbia has long been mired (stuck) in controversy. Even before the district was created, politicians argued over where to put the nation's capital. Prior to the American Revolution (1775–1783), every meeting of representatives from the various colonies had occurred in Philadelphia, Pennsylvania. At that time it was the largest and richest city in the colonies.

During the Revolutionary War, however, British troops repeatedly drove the fledgling (recently born) American government from the city. Not long after the war, in June 1783, representatives of the newly-formed Confederation Congress were actually captured by a band of American soldiers. The soldiers stormed the meeting and demanded to be paid. Determined to leave Philadelphia, the Congress temporarily relocated to New York City. From 1781 to 1789, America's government operated under the Articles of Confederation. The lack of a permanent capital was just one of the government's many weaknesses.

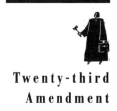

Twenty-third Amendment

Establishing the capital

American statesmen gathered at the Federal Convention of 1787 to write a new plan, or constitution, for governing the nation. One of the most troubling questions they faced was how to establish a national capital. One of the things that most of the framers (authors of the Constitution) agreed on was that, unlike many other nations, the United States would not locate their capital in the most powerful and populous city. They did not want to favor one state over another by locating the capital in that state. Instead, they decided to create an independent district. This would be the home of the federal government. Article I, Section 8, Clause 7 of the Constitution gives Congress the power:

> **To exercise exclusive Legislation in all Cases whatsoever, over such District (not exceeding ten Miles square) as may, by Cession of particular States, and the Acceptance of Congress, become the Seat of the Government of the United States, and to exercise like Authority over all Places purchased by the Consent of the Legislature of the State in which the Same shall be, for the Erection of Forts, Magazines, Arsenals, dock-Yards and other needful Buildings....**

A SLEEPY TOWN ON THE POTOMAC. The Federal Convention ended, and the new federal government was created in 1789. Except, there was one decision left unmade: where to locate the nation's capital. The government operated temporarily from New York City. Representatives from the various states vied (competed) for the opportunity to locate the capi-

tal near them. There was a great deal at stake in the decision. Even though the federal government at the time was small by today's standards, the new capital would need government buildings, hotels and restaurants, roads, and a variety of services. Whoever "got" the nation's capital would receive a financial windfall.

In the end, the capital was chosen in a political compromise between those who favored a strong federal government, the Federalists, and those who favored a weaker central government, the Anti-Federalists. In what became known as the Compromise of 1790, the Anti-Federalists agreed to support Federalist Alexander Hamilton's plan. Hamilton suggested increasing the strength of the federal government in exchange for moving the capital from New York City to Philadelphia for a period of ten years. After that, the capital would then permanently be located somewhere along the banks of the Potomac River, near the home of newly elected president, George Washington.

The "chosen territory," as it was first called, was located on ten square miles that lay between the states of Virginia and Maryland. The Potomac River proved an important route to tobacco markets. The future construction of a canal promised access to the vast interior that was rapidly being populated. The location was thought of as being Southern, but it was located roughly in the center of the string of colonies that lined the Atlantic Ocean. The main city in the district would be renamed Washington in 1800, after the death of the first president. Because of the small size of the district and the growth of Washington city, the city and the district became one and the same.

Building and Rebuilding A City

In Philadelphia, President Washington and Secretary of State Thomas Jefferson negotiated with French-born architect Pierre-Charles L'Enfant to devise a plan for the new city. L'Enfant had been a volunteer in the Revolution, and his commitment to democracy was unwavering.

L'Enfant designed a city with broad avenues laid out in a complex geometric pattern. The various seats of government—the Capitol, the Supreme Court, the Library of Congress, and the Executive Mansion (later named the White House)—all lay in pleasing relationship to each other around a wide park-like area known as the Mall. The government made the move to their new capital in 1800. The nation's second president, John Adams, became the first leader to take up residence in the Executive Mansion.

Not everyone was thrilled with their new capital. Abigail Adams, the first First Lady to occupy the Executive Mansion, called the town "the very dirtiest Hole I ever saw for a place of any trade or respectability of inhabitants." By 1808, the population of the capital was a mere 5,000 residents. Flimsy wooden buildings and muddy roads coexisted alongside the grand federal buildings.

Many complained that the capital was remote and difficult to get to. Others complained of the terribly hot and humid summers in the area. This led many of the residents and most government officials to live elsewhere during the hot summer months. These complaints would eventually be addressed by improvements in transportation and the invention of air conditioning. However, they helped keep Washington, D.C., a small town well into the nineteenth century.

Wartime interference

In 1814, the capital was temporarily abandoned because of an invasion by British soldiers under the leadership of Admiral Sir George Cockburn. Cockburn eventually ordered the burning of the Capitol, the White House, and the Navy Arsenal. If Cockburn thought that he was destroying the seat of the federal government, he was gravely mistaken.

Despite the fact that his actions had little effect on the outcome of the War of 1812, they had a great symbolic outcome on the future of the capital city. What had once been thought of as a place ill suited for governing the nation became a site where foreign powers had attempted to destroy the very heart of the nation. The attack on the capital helped Americans learn to value their capital. The federal government went to extreme measures to protect it from Confederate forces during the Civil War (1861–1865).

Governing the City

By the mid-nineteenth century, most Americans were comfortable with Washington, D.C., as the seat of their government. Many had even begun to grow proud of their nation's capital. But most Americans didn't have to experience the troubled governance of this odd political creation that was neither state nor territory.

The same constitutional clause that allowed for the district's creation also allowed Congress to determine how the district would be governed. At first, the district was governed in a fairly straightforward way. In 1802, Congress granted the city a charter that established a mayor (to be appoint-

*The White House is
a well-known symbol
of the American
capital.* Reproduced by
permission of the National
Park Services.

ed by the president), and a city council (to be elected by the citizens). Ten years later, Congress authorized the city council to choose the mayor. In 1820, they approved the election of a mayor by direct popular vote. This system, called "home rule," was the norm until after the Civil War.

Civil War years

During the Civil War, the city of Washington, D.C., grew in both size and importance. The city became the focal point for the Union war effort. President Abraham Lincoln met with his generals in the city, and much of the military bureaucracy was centered there. Because of its growing importance, Washington, D.C., became the target of Confederate military strategy during the war, but the rebels never succeeded in capturing the city. After the war, the city continued to be the nerve center for federal efforts to rebuild the Union. Even though it was still a small city that shrunk dramatically in the hot summers, Washington, D.C., was growing in importance.

The district's government changes

Congress recognized the district's changing nature. In 1871, Congress changed the district's form of governance to resemble that of a territory. The

district would have a two-house legislative body. The lower house would be chosen by the people. The upper house, the governor, and the board of public works would be appointed by the president. The district would also gain a non-voting delegate to the federal Congress. Within three years, however, this new government had become so caught up in scandal that Congress reversed course dramatically (see sidebar on page 442).

COMMISSION GOVERNMENT. In 1874, Congress ended home rule and reorganized the District's government yet again. Congressional committees became the lawmaking bodies for the district. Soon, however, prominent citizens of the city urged Congress to extend some control back to the city's citizens—or at least to those wealthy and powerful citizens who wanted to increase construction of federal buildings in the district.

Under the Organic Act of 1878, Congress agreed to place the district's executive power in the hands of a three-member board of commissioners. But those commissioners had to report directly to Congress, which retained final say in all matters. Congress also agreed to pay for half of the local government's expenditures (this number dropped to one-third in 1913).

This plan remained in effect until 1967. The citizens of the district had virtually no say in the way they were governed. They could not elect commissioners, Congressman, or the president. In a country where the right to vote was deemed a crucial element of citizenship, the residents of the District of Columbia were at the mercy of rulers they could not choose.

Modern City, Modern Troubles

Through the late nineteenth and into the mid-twentieth century, Washington, D.C., changed dramatically. First, the racial makeup of the city shifted. Nearly 40,000 freed slaves moved to the city following the end of the Civil War. The black population continued to increase into the twentieth century. By the middle of the twentieth-century, the city was 70 percent black. The growth of the federal government during the 1930s and 1940s also swelled the size of the city, and turned it into a major metropolis. By 1960, the capital had a population of over 750,000 people.

The rapid growth and changing racial makeup of the city soon revealed problems with the governing structure set in place in 1878. The main problem was that the District of Columbia was ruled by people who were distinctly uninterested in the concerns of its population. The Congressional committees that ran the district were dominated by white

MISMANAGING THE DISTRICT: THE CASE OF ALEXANDER SHEPHERD

In 1871, the U.S. Congress reshaped the federal capital's government, Washington, D.C., to make it more like the territories that lined the nation's western frontiers. In addition to one elected legislative body, the district now had an appointed upper house, governor, and commissioner of public works. The district's first commissioner of public works, Alexander Shepherd, was appointed by President Ulysses S. Grant. Within a few years, Shepherd had bankrupted the district, and forced Congress to reclaim government control.

Shepherd had grand dreams for the nation's capital. He wanted to make it a place of which the nation could truly be proud. He soon began following through on his ambitious plans. He paved streets, planted trees, installed a sewer system and a system of gas-fired street lights. For a time, it looked like he would succeed. But as Shepherd began to submit bills to Congress to pay for all these improvements, the entire scheme unraveled.

Shepherd had spent more than $20 million to improve the city—more than three times what he told Congress he would need. Government accountants searched his financial records, but could not determine what happened to large sums of money. Soon Shepherd faced a Congressional investigation into his wrongdoing. He was unwilling to endure the public shame of the scandal, and fled to Mexico. In the wake of the scandal, Congress took control of the district's government and retained it until 1967.

Southern congressmen. The commissioners were chosen from among the rich, white landowners and businessmen of the city. The city's lawmakers did not understand, or care about, the problems facing the city's black population. Nor did they want to engage in the complexities of governing this major city.

The difficulties faced by the district's citizens were clear. Though they lived in a land that boasted it was the birthplace of democracy, citizens of the nation's capital had no representation. As Kris Palmer writes in *Constitutional Amendments,* "the people of the city where the president of the United States lived and worked while he held office had no role in choosing him." It was clear to many that something had to change.

A time for change

The changing social and cultural climate of the mid-twentieth century provided an opportunity for the district's citizens to gain voting rights. Women had gained voting rights with the passage of the Nineteenth Amendment in 1920. Throughout the South, participants in the emerging civil rights movement were trying to force America to live up to its ideals of freedom and equality.

By 1954, the movement had gained a major victory with the Supreme Court's ruling in *Brown v. Board of Education.* The practical outcome of the decision was the abolishing of school segregation as a violation of the Equal Protection Clause of the Fourteenth Amendment. But its greater impact was on a symbolic level. The Supreme Court had declared that institutionalized racism would no longer be protected by the law of the land.

CIVIL RIGHTS. The civil rights movement placed real emphasis on voting rights. Members insisted that it was unacceptable to let the white-dominated governments found in many Southern states manipulate the law to keep African Americans from registering to vote. They pushed to remove voting obstacles, such as literacy tests and the poll tax. These obstacles ran counter to the Fourteenth Amendment's Equal Protection Clause, the Fifteenth Amendment, and various federal civil rights laws. Residents of the District of Columbia took advantage of this concern with voting rights. They offered themselves as an example of American citizens who had virtually no power of self-governance. In fact, their influence over local politics was largely restricted to voting in school board elections.

Strange Path to An Amendment

A concern with voting rights fueled the eventual passage of an amendment that granted the citizens of the District the right to vote for the president and vice president. However, the proposal that became the Twenty-third Amendment was first associated with the fear that America's enemies might bomb the capital. Thus leaving the nation without a government. It was a strange path for an amendment to follow.

Twenty-third Amendment

Tensions between the Soviet Union and the United States ran high in the long period of American history known as the Cold War (1947–1989). Some politicians worried that a nuclear bomb attack on Washington, D.C., would paralyze the nation. In February 1960, Senator Estes Kefauver introduced a resolution. He proposed a constitutional amendment that would authorize state governors to appoint temporary representatives and senators in the event of an emergency.

Seeing an opportunity, Senator Spessard Holland added a clause to Kefauver's amendment that would eliminate the poll tax. Finally, Senator Kenneth B. Keating added a third clause to the amendment. This clause called for giving the District of Columbia seats in the House of Representatives, and presidential electoral votes based on population. The Senate approved the three part amendment seventy to eighteen and sent it to the House.

Representative Emmanuel Celler, chair of the House Judiciary Committee, believed the amendment was too broad to gain the approval of the House. Celler was a wise politician. He realized that it was not the right time to pursue the broad proposal put forth by his three colleagues. He thought that the only proposal that had a chance of approval was a much narrower one. One aimed only at granting the District of Columbia three electoral votes, a number that was no more than the least populous state in the union as outlined in the Twelfth Amendment. Celler promised to pursue the poll tax amendment in the next congressional session. He offered the House the D.C. voting rights amendment, and received their approval on June 14, 1960. Senate members complained about the pared down amendment, but they approved it two days later and sent it on to the states.

Sectional ratification

Hawaii and Massachusetts quickly approved the amendment, but most other state legislatures were on their summer recesses. The amendment was not approved in time for citizens of the district to vote in the 1960 presidential election. Once the state legislatures returned from their recesses, they quickly set about ratifying the amendment. By March 29, 1961, the amendment had been approved by the required three-fourths of states.

The speed with which the amendment was ratified did not reflect the nation's deep divisions concerning the amendment. Northern and western states all lined up behind the amendment, but most southern states felt that the amendment was an attack on states' rights. After all, they reasoned, the District of Columbia was not a state. Therefore, it

The re-election of President Lyndon B. Johnson in 1964 was the first election that the citizens of Washington, D.C., were able to vote in. Reproduced by permission of AP/Wide World Photos.

should not be afforded the rights of statehood. Ten southern states refused to act on the amendment at all. An eleventh, Arkansas, rejected it outright. Accusations of racism tainted the southern reaction to the amendment. Many felt that white politicians in the South resented the fact that a heavily populated African American area was to be given three electoral votes.

The Impact of the Twenty-third Amendment

The Twenty-third Amendment was a major victory both for voting rights advocates and for the citizens of the District of Columbia. Within the district, the amendment was followed by attempts to return to some form of home rule. In 1966, President Lyndon B. Johnson issued an executive order giving himself the power to appoint a mayor and city council. It was the first major change in city government since 1878. In 1971, Congress extended the district the right to elect a nonvoting delegate to the House of Representatives.

Finally, in 1973, Congress passed a Home Rule Act. This gave the district more control than it had ever enjoyed over its administration. The mayor and city council were elected by the people, but Congress could still exercise veto power. The Home Rule Act created a balance of power between the people who lived in the district, and the federal government that called the district its home.

Continued challenges

Home rule for the District of Columbia has not been without its problems, however. The city administration was troubled by fiscal irresponsibility that became glaringly obvious in the 1980s and 1990s. Additionally, various scandals involving prominent officials, like Mayor Marion Barry, have done little to gain the Congress's confidence in the district's ability to govern itself. In fact, in the mid-1990s, Congress imposed strict fiscal regulations on the district's budget. Many local politicians feared that they would lose home rule if fundamental improvements were not made.

Many within the district would still like to see local citizen's exercise more control, and

Various scandals involving prominent Washington, D.C., officials, such as Mayor Marion Barry, have caused Congress to review the administration of the city. Reproduced by permission of AP/Wide World Photos.

gain representation in Congress. These people led a movement in the late 1970s to acquire all the rights of statehood for the district. The amendment was sent to the states by Congress, but most states believed that passing it was not in their best interests. The amendment went unratified (see sidebar on page 447).

The statehood amendment may have failed, but the district has made its influence felt during the election of presidential candidates. Ever since the ratification of the Twenty-third Amendment, the district's three electoral votes have gone for Democratic presidential candidates. This confirmed the fears of conservatives who believed that granting the district electoral votes amounted to giving away power.

THE PUSH FOR D.C. STATEHOOD:
A FAILED AMENDMENT

Advocates of voting rights for the citizens of the District of Columbia gained a major victory with the passage of the Twenty-third Amendment, but they still complained that citizens lacked the full representation they deserved. What was needed, they argued, was a constitutional amendment giving the district all the benefits of a state. Backers of D.C. statehood began to push for such an amendment in the late 1970s.

After a significant period of debate, Congress approved the following amendment by a vote of 289-127 in the House, and 67-32 in the Senate:

> *Section 1. For purposes of representation in the Congress, election of the President and Vice President, and article V of this Constitution, the District constituting the seat of government of the United States shall be treated as though it were a State.*

> *Section 2. The exercise of the rights and powers conferred under this article shall be done by the people of the District constituting the seat of government, and as shall be provided by the Congress.*

> *Section 3. The twenty-third article of amendment to the Constitution of the United States is hereby repealed.*

> *Section 4. This article shall be inoperative, unless it shall have been ratified as an amendment to the Constitution by the legislatures of three-fourths of the several States within seven years from the date of its submission.*

By the end of the seven-year ratification deadline in 1985, only 16 states had ratified the amendment. The remainder of the states had either rejected it, or simply ignored it. The D.C. statehood amendment died. Today, the citizens of the District of Columbia still remain without adequate representation at the federal level. But thanks to the Twenty-third Amendment, they can cast votes in presidential elections.

**Twenty-third
Amendment**

Despite the Twenty-third Amendment, the District of Columbia remains an unusual entity, a city without a state. Its residents have the unusual privilege of assuming some of the obligations of citizenship (such as paying income tax), while being denied others (such as the right to elect representatives in Congress). Yet, it seems unlikely that we will ever see an amendment that changes this unusual status.

For More Information

Books

Bernstein, Richard B. and Jerome Agel. *Amending America: If We Love the Constitution So Much, Why Do We Keep Trying to Change It?* Lawrence, KS: University Press of Kansas, 1995.

Bowling, Kenneth R. *Creating Washington, D.C.: Potomac Fever.* Washington, D.C.: American Institute of Architects, 1988.

Diner, Steven J. *Democracy, Federalism, and the Governance of the Nation's Capital, 1790-1974.* Washington, D.C.: Center for Applied Research and Urban Policy, 1987.

Feinberg, Barbara S. *The Amendments.* New York: Henry Holt, 1996.

Kyvig, David. *Explicit and Authentic Acts: Amending the U.S. Constitution, 1776–1995.* Lawrence, KS: University of Kansas Press, 1996.

Morin, Isobel V. *Our Changing Constitution: How and Why We Have Amended It.* Brookfield, CT: Millbrook Press, 1998.

Palmer, Kris E., editor. *Constitutional Amendments, 1789 to the Present.* Detroit, MI: Gale Group, 2000.

Web Sites

District of Columbia Home Rule Charter Review. "The District of Columbia as a National Capital and the District of Columbia as a Place to Live: A History of Local Governance to Present Day." [Online] http://www.georgetown.edu/grad/gppp/Community/Publications/history.htm (accessed August 2000).

"U.S. Constitution: Twenty-Third Amendment." [Online] http://caselaw.findlaw.com/data/constitution/amendment23/ (accessed August 10, 2000).

Twenty-fourth Amendment

SECTION 1. The right of citizens of the United States to vote in any primary or other election for President or Vice President, for electors for President or Vice President, or for Senator or Representative in Congress, shall not be denied or abridged by the United States or any State by reason of failure to pay any poll tax or other tax.

SECTION 2. The Congress shall have power to enforce this article by appropriate legislation.

The Constitution of the United States describes in detail a government of elected officials, but it does not set out clear rules for who may vote in elections. In an effort to clarify this vagueness, several amendments have been passed to ensure that the right to vote is not limited unfairly. The Twenty-fourth Amendment clearly forbids the federal government or any state government from requiring that voters pay any kind of fee before they can vote.

This was a necessary amendment to the Constitution. In the decades following the end of the Civil War (1861–1865), the southern states used unfair election practices to prevent African American voters from exercising their right to vote. One of the most effective practices was the poll tax. Beginning with Georgia in 1875, southern legislatures passed poll tax laws that were specifically designed "so that ... the Negro shall never be heard from again," in the words of Georgia politician Robert Toombs, as quoted in *Constitutional Amendments:1789 to the Present.* By 1910, poll taxes were on the books in Georgia, Mississippi, Texas, Virginia, North Carolina, South Carolina, Alabama, Louisiana, Florida, Arkansas, and Tennessee—all the states that had formerly seceded (separated) from the Union, and called themselves the Confederate States of America.

Twenty-fourth Amendment

RATIFICATION FACTS

PROPOSED: Submitted by Congress to the states on August 27, 1962.

RATIFICATION: Ratified by the required three-fourths of states (thirty-eight of fifty) on January 23, 1964, and by one more state on February 25, 1977. Declared to be part of the Constitution on February 4, 1964.

RATIFYING STATES: Illinois, November 14, 1962; New Jersey, December 3, 1962; Oregon, January 25, 1963; Montana, January 28, 1963; West Virginia, February 1, 1963; New York, February 4, 1963; Maryland, February 6, 1963; California, February 7, 1963; Alaska, February 11, 1963; Rhode Island, February 14, 1963; Indiana, February 19, 1963; Utah, February 20, 1963; Michigan, February 20, 1963; Colorado, February 21, 1963; Ohio, February 27, 1963; Minnesota, February 27, 1963; New Mexico, March 5, 1963; Hawaii, March 6, 1963; North Dakota, March 7, 1963; Idaho, March 8, 1963; Washington, March 14, 1963; Vermont, March 15, 1963; Nevada, March 19, 1963; Connecticut, March 20, 1963; Tennessee, March 21, 1963; Pennsylvania, March 25, 1963; Wisconsin, March 26, 1963; Kansas, March 28, 1963; Massachusetts, March 28, 1963; Nebraska, April 4, 1963; Florida, April 18, 1963; Iowa, April 24, 1963; Delaware, May 1, 1963; Missouri, May 13, 1963; New Hampshire, June 12, 1963; Kentucky, June 27, 1963; Maine, January 16, 1964; South Dakota, January 23, 1964; Virginia, February 25, 1977.

The roots of the southern poll tax lie in the deep divisions between whites and blacks that began with the practice of slavery. These divisions continued even after the end of the Civil War, when several constitutional amendments were passed. The amendments ended slavery, and granted black males the right to vote. Southern whites were afraid of the political power (and possibly the anger) of the newly freed blacks. They took extreme steps to limit that power. But it was not only in the South that racism was at work. The United States Supreme Court rejected challenge after challenge to the poll tax laws of the South. It took the Civil Rights movement of the 1950s and 1960s to pass lasting legislation against the discriminatory poll tax—almost one hundred years after poll taxes started.

After Slavery: From Reconstruction to the Black Codes

To understand the importance of the Twenty-fourth Amendment, it is important to understand the society from which it grew. This story begins with the end of slavery. Once the Civil War was over, U.S. legislators realized that the end of the war was only the beginning of their work to bring the nation back together.

The period from the end of the war in 1865 to 1877 was called the Reconstruction era. Reconstruction means rebuilding, and the Reconstruction era was a period of rebuilding the South on several levels. On the physical level, much of the land and many of the buildings in the South had been destroyed by the terrible fighting. Cities and farms had to be rebuilt. On the political level, the South had to develop a new economy that did not depend on slavery. The states that had withdrawn from the Union had to be readmitted into the United States. The country had to figure out a way to reunite in peacetime, and this newly reunited nation had almost four million new citizens—the freed slaves.

Congress quickly proposed three new amendments to the Constitution in order to define the status of the black Americans who were no longer enslaved. Between 1865 and 1870, the Fourteenth, Fifteenth and Sixteenth Amendments were ratified. These amendments gave former slaves the status of citizenship, equality under the law, and the right to vote.

Southern governments reorganize

Having survived generations of slavery where they had few rights, the new African American citizens were ready and eager to exercise their new rights to vote and to hold office. White Northerners who had moved south were called carpetbaggers, because of their cloth suitcases. They teamed up with white Southern Republicans (called scalawags by Southern Democrats), and the new black voters to reorganize the governments of the Southern states.

Republicans quickly voted out the traditional Democratic politicians of the South. This created radical Republican governments that included black representatives for the first time. By 1868, these new governments had set up a public school system, along with other social services. They also established the Freedmen's Bureau to safeguard the rights of black Americans. Interracial governments started functioning productively, especially in Mississippi, South Carolina, and Louisiana. These new governments looked remarkably different from previous

Southern governments. By 1870, for instance, there were 30 black state representatives and 5 black senators in the state of Mississippi.

THE OLD SOUTH RESPONDS. Unfortunately, white Southerners were angry and frightened by the enormous changes to their way of life. The South had just suffered a bitter defeat in one of the most tragic wars in history. The sudden changes of Reconstruction seemed like one more humiliating defeat, especially for the landowners who had lost a great deal during the war. It infuriated them to lose their power. Seeing that power in the hands of their former slaves and "Yankees" (as they called Northerners) made them even more resentful.

During the centuries of slave-owning, white landowners had convinced themselves that blacks were not really people. This is one reason why they did not easily accept the new citizens as their equals. With what political power they had left, they began to enact laws they called "black codes" in the 1870s. These codes were aimed at keeping black Southerners second-class citizens. To enforce white supremacy, whites organized themselves into secret societies like the Ku Klux Klan and the Society of the White Rose. These groups tried to frighten blacks with threats and physical violence. For example, in 1869, white Democrats in Mobile, Alabama, aimed a cannon at black citizens who were lined up to vote, forcing them to run for their lives.

By 1877, these tactics of suppression, threats, and violence had worked. Northern support for African Americans dwindled. The U.S. Supreme Court overruled much of the civil rights legislation that the radical Republicans had passed. The Democrats who had been booted out of Southern legislatures were elected again, as whites once more controlled the elections. In turn, these legislators enacted laws that cut the rights of black Americans almost back to slavery. The new governments where black and white legislators worked together were gone. Though no longer slaves, blacks had little economic or political power. And the new laws were meant to ensure that things stayed that way.

Jim Crow and the Loss of the Vote

In their effort to make sure black Americans were unable to gain equal status with whites, white Southerners used two approaches. One was segregation. This meant making laws that prevented black and white Americans from using the same public services or facilities. This led to separate train cars, bathrooms, water fountains, etc., for whites and blacks. These laws, and segregation itself, were nicknamed "Jim Crow" after a stereotypical black character in a minstrel show. Segregation kept whites and blacks apart, limited what kinds of facilities were available to blacks, and reinforced the Southern notion that the races were fundamentally different. This approach also drove a wedge between poor white Southerners and blacks, who might otherwise have had much in common.

The other approach to keeping power in white hands was to keep blacks from voting. When the Fifteenth Amendment was ratified, the Southern states could not take the vote away. But they could—and did—create new laws that made it almost impossible for black citizens to cast their vote.

Many of the states actually rewrote their constitutions just to add obstacles that prevented large numbers of African Americans from voting. The new laws often demanded literacy tests for voters, and many blacks could not read. There were other approaches to limiting black voting rights, such as holding primaries to pick candidates where only whites could vote, or grandfather clauses that stated a person could only vote if they had been able to vote before the Fifteenth Amendment. By far, the most effective obstacle to black suffrage, or voting, was the poll tax.

The poll tax

The poll tax of the late 1800s and early 1900s, as applied by white Southern state governments, was different than other forms of poll tax. Its specific purpose was not to raise revenue, but to prevent black voters from gaining political power.

This is how the poll tax worked: state law required each voting citizen to pay a tax, from one to several dollars a year, depending on the state. The tax had to be paid at least six months before an election. At election time, each voter had to show a receipt to prove that he or she had paid the tax, not only for that year but for preceding years as well. Though the tax was low, it represented a considerable amount for poor working people. What was worse, if a citizen did not pay the tax one year, the state added penalties and interest. This meant that by the next year the fee was much higher. Voters who had not paid for several years would face a tax that had grown to an amount they could never afford to pay. And if they could not come up with the money, they could not vote.

The Southern poll tax was an extremely regressive tax. That is, it affected poor people much more than the wealthy. As such, it affected poor whites too, and sometimes prevented them from voting. When politicians needed more votes, however, they could "buy" white votes by

POLL TAXES: NOT ALWAYS AT THE POLLS

In the United States, the poll tax has long been associated with voting, but it actually had nothing to do with voting when it began. The word poll comes from Middle English, and, before that, from a Danish word meaning the crown of the head. The poll tax, therefore, was simply a head tax, or a tax that everyone paid simply for living in the area that was taxed. American usage of the word "polls" for the place people vote also comes from the idea of counting heads. But until the nineteenth century, the poll tax was not related to voting.

Throughout history, poll taxes have been used by many governments to raise money. In addition, they were also sometimes used to penalize people who were not part of the ruling group. As far back as the Greek and Roman empires, people who had been conquered by the empire were forced to pay a head tax. From 1691 until 1839, the Ottoman Turks levied a poll tax on all non-Muslim people within the huge Ottoman Empire.

simply paying their poll taxes for them. By 1910, eleven of the Southern states used a poll tax, among other devices, to interfere with black voters. They succeeded remarkably well. One example shows the devastating effect of the new laws on black suffrage. In 1900, Richmond, Virginia, had 6,427 black voters. By 1907, the number had dropped to 228.

Trying to Defeat the Poll Tax

As blatantly unfair as using devices like the poll tax to prevent black Americans from voting seems today, bitter white Southerners were not the only ones who supported these bigoted laws. Time after time, when black citizens and others challenged the legality of the poll tax, the United States Supreme Court upheld the states' rights to have such a tax. In general, the Federal Court was reluctant to limit the powers of the states. For almost sixty years the Supreme Court maintained that setting the rules about who could vote was a power that belonged to the individual states. Several courts agreed that since everyone had to pay the poll tax, it was not a discriminatory tax—even if it was used in a discriminatory way. The poll tax remained in place all over the South for decades.

Also in many European countries, the poll tax was an important source of revenue up to the 1800s. Even then, the tax was considered unfair by many people. Placing the same tax on everyone's "head" is considered regressive. That is, poor people must pay the same tax as rich people, even though it is much harder for them to come up with the money. As a result of this, poor people have often protested when they have been ordered to pay a poll tax.

When Richard II of England imposed a poll tax, he lit the fuse that started the bloody Peasants' Revolt of 1381. During this revolt, four of the king's ministers were beheaded. Almost three centuries later, in 1649, King Charles I lost his head for many unpopular taxation policies—among them, the hated poll tax. Still, British governments have continued to levy poll taxes, even up to the present day. In 1990, Prime Minister Margaret Thatcher began a new poll tax that set off riots in London, and inspired wide-scale tax resistance in Scotland.

President Franklin D. Roosevelt spoke out in the 1930s against the Southern poll taxes. In *Constitutional Amendments: 1789 to the Present*, President Roosevelt referred to them as "contrary to fundamental democracy." However, presidents are politicians as well, and political pressure from the South made Roosevelt soften his opposition to the tax.

Other reformers did work to abolish the tax, however, like white Southerner Virginia Foster Durr. She had helped found the Civil Rights Committee of the Southern Conference for Human Welfare to offer legal advice and support for black voters. Reformers succeeded in getting the poll tax repealed in three states: Florida, Louisiana, and North Carolina. However, in the states that still had the tax, change was slow in coming. Even if reformers managed to propose bills to end the poll tax, Southern legislators could stall bills in Congress by talking and debating endlessly until the session was over. This type of stalling technique is called a filibuster.

The Second Reconstruction

The 1940s brought the United States into World War II (1939–1945). Many changes took place in U.S. politics and attitudes. During the war itself, a

Twenty-fourth Amendment

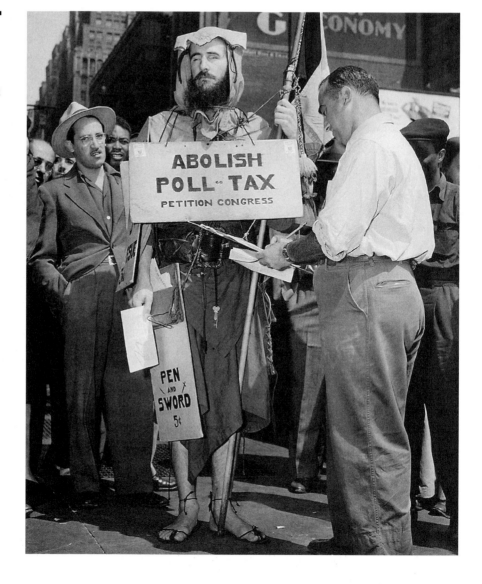

Many prospective African American voters were discouraged by the poll tax. Reproduced by permission of the Corbis Corporation (Bellevue).

blow was struck at the poll tax: the Soldier Vote Act of 1942 allowed soldiers fighting overseas to vote by absentee ballot without paying a poll tax. The war brought other new opportunities to African Americans. They worked in the defense industries, just as whites did. They served in the armed forces, just as whites did. Going abroad, they experienced more open societies. This made it difficult for African Americans to return to their place at the bottom of American society, especially in the segregated South.

Blacks continued to face discrimination and segregation as they worked in the war industries. The flood of black workers going North to work in factories led to fear and hostility. Tensions erupted in race riots. The worst riots were in Detroit, Michigan, in June, 1943.

The armed forces themselves were still segregated, and a ten percent quota limited how many black Americans could serve. With the help of the National Association for the Advancement of Colored People, black citizens worked to persuade President Franklin Roosevelt to eliminate discrimination within the war effort. On June 25, 1941, President Roosevelt signed Executive Order 8802. This established the Fair Employment Practices Commission to lessen discrimination in the war industries, the armed services, and the federal government. But the order was not very effective.

The struggle to end segregation after the war

After the war ended, individual blacks and organizations like the NAACP continued to work to end Jim Crow segregation in the South. Right after the war, and continuing through the 1950s and 1960s, civil rights workers in the South began the struggle to eliminate the obstacles to black suffrage. They held voter registration drives, and helped blacks register to vote, pass literacy tests, and pay their poll taxes. Political activists from the North were inspired by the changes happening in the South. They went to the southern states to offer their help in the movement.

NON-VIOLENT RESISTANCE. Even though angry whites tried to stop them, African American activists and their supporters continued to protest unfair conditions, and worked to win equal rights for black citizens. In fact, much of the civil rights movement's success came about because black Americans responded to white violence with quiet determination and non-violent protests. Black civil rights leaders like Rosa Parks of Alabama, Martin Luther King, Jr. of Georgia, and Bayard Rustin of Pennsylvania encouraged activists to use non-violent resistance. That is, to work for their rights using peaceful tactics. That peaceful fight gained much sympathy for black civil rights across the United States.

ROSA PARKS AND THE MONTGOMERY BUS BOYCOTT. The Montgomery, Alabama, bus boycott is a good example of how non-violent tactics worked. (A boycott is a political tactic where a group of people refuse to use a product or service in order to protest something they don't like about the product or service.) Rosa Parks was a longtime member of the Alabama NAACP. In December 1955, she chose to protest the segregation of buses in Montgomery. Blacks were required by law to sit in the back of buses, and to stand if a white passenger needed their seat. Instead of giving up her seat to a white passenger and moving to the back of the bus,

THE NAACP

The summer of 1908 saw tragic violence in Springfield, Illinois—the former home town of the nation's sixteenth president, Abraham Lincoln (1809–1865). Several days of race riots there ended with the death or injury of dozens of black citizens. Thousands more left Springfield, trying to escape the violence.

Many were overcome with frustration and anger at the treatment of African Americans. Journalist William Walling, social worker and activist Mary White Ovington, and *New York Evening Post* publisher Oswald Garrison Villard called for all believers in democracy to come to a conference to discuss the plight of African Americans. Thousands responded. On May 30, 1909, out of this conference, the National Association for the Advancement of Colored People (NAACP) was born.

Members of the new organization were angry and dismayed over the condition of black citizens. Issues of particular concern were voting rights, segregation, access to education, and violence against blacks. They criticized the South for its repressive policies against blacks. They criticized the North for taking little positive action to help blacks. And they criticized the Supreme Court for refusing to stop the states' abuses. They decided to use their newly-formed organization to help.

The NAACP went to work immediately. Members made public speeches and pressured politicians about equal rights for black Americans. They fought discrimination and segregation through the courts. They started *The Crisis,* a magazine about the issues of civil rights and

Parks did not fight or argue. She simply stayed seated and refused to move. She was arrested and put in jail.

Martin Luther King, Jr. was a minister who had studied non-violent resistance. Bayard Rustin was a political organizer who had learned about non-violence from his Quaker grandparents. They heard of Parks' action and began to organize a boycott of the Montgomery buses. Instead of fighting or responding with anger, the black citizens of Montgomery simply refused to ride the bus. Those blacks who rode the bus were often poor and may have seemed powerless, but the bus company needed the money that they paid to ride the bus. The boycott was also a dramatic way

discrimination. The magazine was edited for years by the black leader, W.E.B. Du Bois.

One of the NAACP's first goals was to stop racial violence, especially lynching. A lynching is to execute someone without due process of law, often by hanging. Blacks were often lynched by angry mobs of whites for either real or imagined crimes. In 1911, as the NAACP was getting started, there were 71 lynchings across the United States—63 of them killing blacks. The NAACP focused American attention on the barbaric violence of lynch mobs by holding silent demonstrations, placing large newspaper ads, and using political pressure, even on the president. Lynchings decreased, and by 1950, had stopped almost entirely.

In 1920, James Weldon Johnson became the NAACP's first black executive secretary. Johnson expanded the organization's membership in the South. Under his leadership, membership grew to ninety thousand. Johnson served until 1930. He was followed by Walter White, who served until 1955. Together, Johnson and White increased the influence and strength of the NAACP until it became the most powerful and best-known civil rights organization in the country.

The NAACP is still active and growing. In 1999, it had over 500,000 members in 2,200 chapters in the United States, Japan, and Germany. The NAACP still finds much inequality to combat. On its web site, its goals are: "to ensure the political, educational, social and economic equality of minority group citizens of the United States and eliminate race prejudice."

to publicize the cause of civil rights across the nation. It was not easy for poor people who did not own cars not to ride the bus. It took a whole year, but on December 20, 1956, the Supreme Court forced the bus company to change its policy of discrimination and integrate the Montgomery buses.

Opening the way for the poll tax amendment

The civil rights movement continued to win other important political victories. In *Brown v. the Board of Education of Topeka, Kansas* (1954), the Supreme Court ruled that segregation of public schools was unconstitutional. This was a big victory for civil rights, because blacks and whites could now attend classes together. It was also a big victory because, for

Twenty-fourth Amendment

Many Southerners angered by the decision in Brown v. Board of Education, *started calling for the impeachment of the Supreme Court's chief justice, Earl Warren.* Courtesy of the Library of Congress.

the first time, the Court had imposed a federal law about the treatment of blacks in the separate states. This finally opened the way to defeating the poll tax that had limited black voting rights for over half a century.

Even with all the changes brought about by the growing civil rights movement, it took several more tries before the bill proposing the abolition of the poll tax finally got to Congress—attached to the end of another bill. Even then, the poll tax amendment was debated and switched from bill to bill for two years. The proposed amendment passed the Senate on March 27, 1962, by a vote of 77 to 16. It passed the House on August 27, 1962, by a vote of 294 to 86, and on that date was sent to the states for ratification. Most Southern states refused to consider the amendment. Only one Southern state—Tennessee—passed it. But Northern states rallied behind it, and the amendment received the thirty-eight state votes needed for ratification in January 1964.

The End Effects of the Poll Tax

The Twenty-Fourth Amendment effectively abolished the poll tax as a way of controlling who votes in elections. By 1966, after a series of

Supreme Court cases, the Court ruled that not only was the poll tax forbidden in federal elections, but that individual states could not require a poll tax for voting in state elections either. This was another case where the federal government now claimed authority where it had once let individual states decide for themselves. Although this angered many, it proved to be the best way to defeat the prejudices that existed in different regions.

The Twenty-fourth Amendment led to civil rights laws, such as the Civil Rights Act of 1964 and the Voting Rights Act of 1965. The Civil Rights Act forbids racial discrimination in education, employment, and use of public facilities. The Voting Rights Act got rid of most of the other state obstacles to black suffrage by abolishing literacy tests, and placing federal examiners in counties where registration of black voters was low.

For More Information

Books

Davidson, Chandler, and Bernard Grofman, editors. *Quiet Revolution in the South: The Impact of the Voting Rights Act 1965-1990.* Princeton, NJ: Princeton University Press, 1994.

Dolan, Sean. *Pursuing the Dream: From the Selma-Montgomery March to the Formation of PUSH.* New York: Chelsea House, 1995.

Dunn, John M. *The Civil Rights Movement.* San Diego, CA: Lucent Books, 1998.

Foner, Eric. *Reconstruction: America's Unfinished Revolution.* New York: Harper and Row, 1988.

Hampton, Henry, with Steve Fayer and Sarah Flynn. *Voices of Freedom: An Oral History of the Civil Rights Movement from the 1950s through the 1980s.* New York: Bantam Books, 1990.

Harris, Jacqueline L. *History and Achievement of the NAACP.* New York: F. Watts, 1992.

Lawson, Steven F. *Black Ballots: Voting Rights in the South, 1944-1969.* Lanham, MA: Lexington Books, 1999.

Palmer, Kris E. *Constitutional Amendments: 1789 to the Present.* Detroit, MI: Gale Group, 2000.

Schmidt, Benno C., Jr. "Principle and Prejudice: The Supreme Court and Race in the Progressive Era." *Columbia Law Review.* June 1982.

**Twenty-fourth
Amendment**

Wells, Ida B. *Crusade for Justice.* Chicago, IL: University of Chicago
Press, 1972.

Articles

Foner, Eric. "Time for a Third Reconstruction." *The Nation.* Vol. 256,
No. 4, February 1, 1993.

Hitchens, Christopher. "Minority Report: Class and the Poll Tax Riots,
Great Britain." *The Nation.* Vol. 250, No. 17, April 30, 1990.

Weisberger, Bernard A. "Amending America." *American Heritage.*
Vol. 46, no. 3, May-June 1995, pp. 24-26.

Web Sites

"NAACP Online." [Online] http://www.naacp.org. (accessed
June 23, 2000).

Twenty-fifth Amendment

SECTION 1. In case of the removal of the President from office or of his death or resignation, the Vice President shall become President.

SECTION 2. Whenever there is a vacancy in the office of the Vice President, the President shall nominate a Vice President who shall take office upon confirmation by a majority vote of both Houses of Congress.

SECTION 3. Whenever the President transmits to the President pro tempore of the Senate and the Speaker of the House of Representatives his written declaration that he is unable to discharge the powers and duties of his office, and until he transmits to them a written declaration to the contrary, such powers and duties shall be discharged by the Vice President as Acting President.

SECTION 4. Whenever the Vice President and a majority of either the principal officers of the executive departments or of such other body as Congress may by law provide, transmit to the President pro tempore of the Senate and the Speaker of the House of Representatives their written declaration that the President is unable to discharge the powers and duties of his office, the Vice President shall immediately assume the powers and duties of the office as Acting President.

Thereafter, when the President transmits to the President pro tempore of the Senate and the Speaker of the House of Representatives his written declaration that no inability exists, he shall resume the powers and duties of his office unless the Vice President and a majority of either the principal officers of the executive departments or of such other body as Congress may by law provide, transmit within four days to the President pro tempore of the Senate and the Speaker of the House of Representatives their written declaration that the President is unable to discharge the powers and duties of his office. Thereupon Congress shall decide the issue, assembling within forty-eight hours for that purpose if not in session. If the Congress, within twenty-one

days after receipt of the latter written declaration, or, if Congress is not in session, within twenty-one days after Congress is required to assemble, determines by two-thirds vote of both Houses that the President is unable to discharge the powers and duties of his office, the Vice President shall continue to discharge the same as Acting President; otherwise, the President shall resume the powers and duties of his office.

The Constitution anticipated many of the problems that would face the United States, but it did not spell out exactly what should happen if a president had to leave office in the middle of his term, either permanently or temporarily. For almost 200 years, questions about presidential succession were answered on an as needed basis by the administration in office. Though the need for rules specifying the process of presidential succession were evident when President George Washington fell gravely ill during his first term in office, the Twenty-fifth Amendment was not added to the Constitution until 1967.

The basic goal of the Twenty-fifth Amendment is to ensure the smooth transition of power from a president leaving office mid-term to another who will assume his position. A president may leave office for a variety of reasons. The Twenty-fifth Amendment's four sections establish rules for the various reasons that a government might need to replace the president.

The first section states that when a president dies in office, resigns, or is impeached that the vice president will become the president for the remainder of the departing president's term of office. The second section details how the president may fill a vice president's vacant office. These rules were clearly needed. By the year 2000, nine of the forty-two presidents, and eighteen of the forty-five vice presidents, did not complete their terms of office.

Sections three and four of the Twenty-fifth Amendment ensure that the presidency does not remain vacant when the president is temporarily unable to perform his or her responsibilities of office. Section three allows a president to declare himself temporarily unable to function as president, and to indicate that his responsibilities will be assumed by the vice president for a period of time. This section has been used by modern presidents for short periods of time, such as during surgeries when a

RATIFICATION FACTS

PROPOSED: Submitted by Congress to the states on July 6, 1965.

RATIFICATION: Ratified by the required three-fourths of states (thirty-eight of fifty) on February 10, 1967, and by nine more states on May 25, 1967. Declared to be part of the Constitution on February 23, 1967.

RATIFYING STATES: Nebraska, July 12, 1965; Wisconsin, July 13, 1965; Oklahoma, July 16, 1965; Massachusetts, August 9, 1965; Pennsylvania, August 18, 1965; Kentucky, September 15, 1965; Arizona, September 22, 1965; Michigan, October 5, 1965; Indiana, October 20, 1965; California, October 21, 1965; Arkansas, November 4, 1965; New Jersey, November 29, 1965; Delaware, December 7, 1965; Utah, January 17, 1966; West Virginia, January 20, 1966; Maine, January 24, 1966; Rhode Island, January 28, 1966; Colorado, February 3, 1966; New Mexico, February 3, 1966; Kansas, February 8, 1966; Vermont, February 10, 1966; Alaska, February 18, 1966; Idaho, March 2, 1966; Hawaii, March 3, 1966; Virginia, March 8, 1966; Mississippi, March 10, 1966; New York, March 14, 1966; Maryland, March 23, 1966; Missouri, March 30, 1966; New Hampshire, June 13, 1966; Louisiana, July 5, 1966; Tennessee, January 12, 1967; Wyoming, January 25, 1967; Washington, January 26, 1967; Iowa, January 26, 1967; Oregon, February 2, 1967; Minnesota, February 10, 1967; Nevada, February 10, 1967.

president was under general anesthesia. Section four ensures that the United States will not have to be ruled by a disabled president who refuses to step aside. Under section four, the vice president and a body of people appointed by Congress may declare a president unfit to serve, perhaps even against his will.

In total, the four sections of the Twenty-fifth Amendment provide the clear guidelines for presidential succession that were missing from the Constitution. While the amendment seems fairly specific, presidents have been reluctant to use the third section. The perception that the president is healthy and vigorous is an integral part of the public's trust in his abilities—a trust presidents have been hesitant to test, even when their own health seemingly demanded it.

What Happens When the President Can't Do the Job?

What happens if a president must leave office in the middle of his term? The original Constitution did not set clear guidelines for this important political transition. It took the Twenty-fifth Amendment, passed in 1967, to address this failing. The framers of the Constitution gave little thought to presidential succession and disability during the Federal Convention of 1787, but the issues did not take long to prove important.

In 1789, during President George Washington's first term in office, he fell ill with a persistent fever, and a painful tumor on his leg. The tumor had to be surgically removed. (Washington was alert during the surgery because anesthesia would not be invented until the 1840s.) Washington quickly regained his health after the surgery, but later the next year he caught a cold that advanced into a near fatal sickness.

These two episodes of presidential illness caused Vice President John Adams much worry about his own position in the government. Article II, Section 1, Clause 6 of the Constitution declared that "In Case of the Removal of the President from Office, or of his Death, Resignation, or Inability to discharge the Powers and Duties of the said Office, the Same shall devolve [pass] on the Vice President." The same article gave Congress the power to determine a successor if both the president and vice president could not serve.

But questions lingered: who would decide that the president was not able to discharge the powers and duties of his office? In the case of the president's inability, would the vice president become the president, or just act in his place? The Constitution did not provide clear answers about how to replace temporarily a disabled president. Adams voiced his concerns to the Senate in 1789, saying "*In esse* I am nothing, but *in posse* I may be everything." Essentially, this means "In this office I am nothing, but I may be everything."

The changing vice presidency

The American government is organized a bit differently today than when John Adams wondered about his duties if the president became disabled. Until the ratification of the Twelfth Amendment in 1804, the vice president was the candidate who came in second in the electoral college votes. He was not a person who campaigned with the presidential candidate, as is the case today. Many times, the president and vice president were political rivals.

After 1804, a vice presidential candidate was often chosen as a running mate. This happened not because he would make a strong president if the president could not fulfill his term, but because he might win votes in an area the presidential candidate could not. The vice presidential candidate would "balance the ticket," or broaden the appeal of the presidential candidate to more voters.

Though not necessarily rivals, the vice president and president might have very different views on government. Vice presidents were rarely included in the president's inner circle of advisers, and had little to do with running the executive office. When the president toured the country or was not in the office to take care of mandatory issues, the president would often leave cabinet members to fulfill his tasks, not the vice president. It has only been in recent times that the vice presidency has been filled by a person with whom the president would want to confer.

Shortly after Washington's illnesses, Congress considered the issues of presidential and vice presidential succession. In 1792, Congress passed the Succession Law that detailed the line of succession from the president, to the vice president, to the president pro tempore of the Senate, and to the Speaker of the House of Representatives. This law left the government vulnerable, however. Congress did not convene until December of the year after elections. Because of this, America risked being without a president or vice president if both offices became vacant when Congress was between sessions.

The Tyler precedent

President William Henry Harrison became the first president to leave office mid-term in 1841. At sixty-eight, Harrison was the oldest man elected to the presidency (a record he held until the election of the seventy-year-old Ronald Reagan in 1981). Eager to prove himself a strong, common man, President Harrison refused to let a driving rain cancel his inaugural speech. During his first few weeks in office, Harrison braved bitter weather as he walked to town to buy his own groceries. He soon caught a cold that quickly turned into pneumonia. Four weeks after his inauguration, President Harrison was dead.

Upon Harrison's death, his vice president, John Tyler, set a precedent (standard) that would be copied until it became section one of the Twenty-fifth Amendment. Tyler became the president. He insisted that the Constitution meant for the vice president to assume the presidency in the case of death. Tyler did not accept the former president's cabinet

Twenty-fifth Amendment

members' pleas to become a passive acting president. Tyler had very different ideas about governing than Harrison, and, for the remainder of Harrison's term, Tyler fought with Congress. He vetoed legislation he thought expanded the authority of the federal government too much.

Harrison's death and the problems of Tyler's rule convinced the Whig Party that they should be more careful the next time they selected a vice president. Tyler had infuriated the Whig party by opposing their agenda after he assumed the presidency.

In 1848, General Zachary Taylor became president. Much like Harrison before him, Taylor was chosen by the Whig Party as a man who would stand behind the party's political agenda. But this time, the Whigs chose a strong supporter of the party's agenda as the vice president. His name was Millard Fillmore. When President Taylor died of a stroke on July 9, 1850, Fillmore followed Tyler's precedent of assuming the presidency. But, unlike Tyler, Fillmore cooperated with the Whig leadership and Taylor's cabinet members for the remainder of his term. Fillmore's positive experience in government helped the Tyler precedent gain validity.

Presidential Death and the Succession Law of 1792

With the assassination of James A. Garfield in 1881, the nation began to debate whether the rules governing the transition of executive power were clear enough. When Garfield campaigned in 1880, there was a deep divide in the Republican party between Stalwarts and Mugwumps. Stalwarts were people comfortable with the spoils system historically used by the Republicans. Mugwumps were those who wanted to make governmental appointments more fair. Generally, Stalwarts used civil offices as rewards for party faithfuls, but Mugwumps despised this practice and pushed for civil-service reform.

Garfield was a Mugwump who ran with a Stalwart, Chester A. Arthur. Arthur was known as the "Gentleman Boss," because of the corruption he presided over as the Collector of Customs of the Port of New York. The Mugwumps who elected Garfield worried that little reform could really happen with a Stalwart in the vice presidency.

The Mugwumps' worst fears were realized when President Garfield was shot by an assassin as he was trying to catch a train in 1881. An angry mob subdued assassin Charles A. Guiteau, who shouted "I am a Stalwart and Arthur is President!" The need for clear rules of transition between a president and a vice president became especially evident as

Garfield lingered for twelve days before dying. Unlike President Abraham Lincoln who died quickly after he was shot sixteen years earlier, Garfield seemed like he might recover. Not wanting to appear eager to take the president's place, Arthur stayed out of Washington until his death. The nation was left without clear leadership for twelve days while doctors searched Garfield's body for the bullet. Garfield died of an infection caused by the doctors' attempts to save him.

As soon as Garfield died, Arthur knew exactly what to do: he assumed the presidency. Surprisingly, as president, Arthur soon reversed his political leanings and won Mugwump praise for supporting civil-service reform. While in office, Arthur's health began to fail him. He suffered from a kidney failing called Bright's disease. Although the disease sapped the president's energy and eventually caused him to suffer bouts of depression, Arthur refused to disclose his condition to the public, and completed his term as president. He had hidden his symptoms so well that his death a year after leaving office shocked many.

Reconsidering the Succession Law

The deaths of presidents and vice presidents concerned many legal scholars. Within the same two decades that Lincoln and Garfield were assassinated, for example, two vice presidents also died. During the second term of Ulysses S. Grant, vice president Henry Wilson died on November 22, 1875, twelve days after suffering a stroke. The president after Arthur, Grover Cleveland, also lost his vice president to a stroke on November 25, 1885. Cleveland did not replace him for most of his first term. The problem was that if the vice president died and the Congress had not yet selected its presiding officers (the speaker of the House of Representatives, and the president pro tempore of the Senate), the nation would only have one top official in office. Should that top official die it was unclear who would lead the country.

To address concerns about presidential succession, Congress passed new legislation in 1886. The new law made the line of succession run from the president and vice president down through the cabinet members, in the order the executive departments they represented had been created. Creators of the law felt it preserved the separation of powers between the legislative branch and the executive branch better than the Succession Law of 1792. In addition, cabinet members were more likely than the leaders of the House or Senate to support the departing president's policies.

This line of succession pertained to the executive branch until 1947 when Harry S Truman assumed the presidency after the death of Franklin

Twenty-fifth Amendment

D. Roosevelt. Shocked by the enormous change in responsibilities of his new office, Truman believed that presidential succession should remain with elected officials. He argued for a new law that looked very much like the Succession Law of 1792. The new statute placed cabinet members after the speaker of the house and the president pro tempore of the Senate in the line of succession. It remains the law of the land into the twenty-first century. The law ensured the country would never be without a leader. But it did not address the process by which the transition of power would take place, nor did it encompass presidential disability.

Harry S. Truman assumed the presidency after the death of Franklin D. Roosevelt. Reproduced by permission of AP/Wide World Photos.

Concealing Presidential Illness

Historically, presidents have tried to conceal their health problems from the public. Presenting themselves as vigorous, strong men, created a public sense of security in their leadership abilities, a sense of security that presidents fear disturbing.

President Grover Cleveland went to extremes to conceal his illness from the public in 1893. Cleveland needed an operation to rid his body of cancer, so he announced that he was going on a yacht trip around Long Island Sound. Secretly, part of the yacht was transformed into a floating operating room where doctors removed cancer from Cleveland's mouth. Though one newspaper caught wind of the story, no one would confirm it.

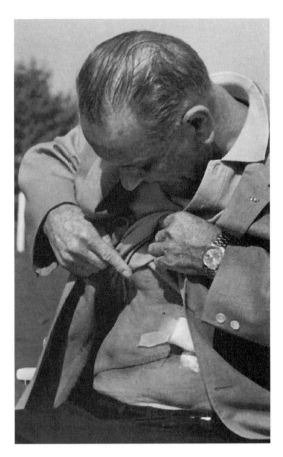

President Lyndon B. Johnson had gall bladder surgery while in office. Reproduced by permission of AP/Wide World Photos.

Only the president's doctors, his family, and close friends were certain of the president's cancer. They did not disclose any information about the operation until 1908, nine years after the president's death.

Over the years, health has become an even more important facet of the presidency. As America developed into the most powerful nation in the world, the responsibilities and demands of the presidency grew too. Once almost a part-time position, the presidency has evolved into one of the most physically and emotionally draining jobs. The public is keenly interested in the president's ability to work under such demanding conditions.

Presidential Disability

The first president to become observably disabled in office was Woodrow Wilson. Wilson was a tough man. He lead the country through the First World War (1914-1918). He was the first American president to travel abroad on official business when he helped to negotiate the Treaty of Versailles at the 1919 Paris Peace Conference.

Even though he was suffering from influenza and severe headaches, Wilson mounted an intense campaign to persuade Congress to ratify the treaty. Wilson planned a rail journey to deliver several speeches a day for twenty-seven days. But the trip proved too much for him. It was canceled on September 26 when Wilson lost movement on the left side of his

body. As he was regaining the movement in his left arm and leg, he suffered a stroke on October 2, 1919. The White House did not offer specific reassurances about the president's health. The public worried that their president had "gone insane and was being kept prisoner in the White House," according to R. B. Bernstein.

The president's cabinet was led by Secretary of State Robert Lansing. He wanted to have the president declared incapacitated, and have the vice president act as president. The legislators looked to the Constitution for guidance, but found it lacking. Wilson's doctor refused to declare Wilson unable to perform the duties of his office. Vice President Thomas R. Marshall did not want to declare himself acting president, because he did not know what would happen if Wilson became ready to assume his duties once more.

Secretary of State Robert Lansing was uncertain about what to do without the leadership of the president, and he was unable to convince Marshall to act as president. Lansing held cabinet meetings without the president, and sometimes without the vice president, between October 1919 and February 1920. The only link to the president during this time was Mrs. Wilson. It was rumored she was running the country during Wilson's illness. On February 7, 1920, President Wilson wrote a punishing letter to Lansing stating that only the president could convene cabinet members under constitutional law. Wilson asked for Lansing's resignation and Lansing complied.

The public was astonished by the news of Lansing's departure. Rumors continued to question the president's mental health. Some members of Congress proposed procedures for determining presidential disability, but secured no action on the issue. Wilson did call cabinet meetings after April 13, 1920, but he never fully regained his health for the rest of his term as president.

Physically-challenged but sharp of mind

Franklin Delano Roosevelt (commonly called FDR) was the first president confined to a wheelchair. Stricken with polio, the president could not stand without help. But many never knew of the president's trouble. The national press corps only released photographs showing the president as the picture of health: portraits or cropped pictures of him standing without his aides.

FDR was a charismatic speaker who inspired many during some of the most difficult times the country had ever faced: the Great Depression

EISENHOWER-NIXON AGREEMENT

Having suffered three debilitating illnesses in office by 1957, President Dwight D. Eisenhower wanted to create rules for the smooth transition of executive power should he suffer another health crisis. Eisenhower, attorney general Herbert Brownell, and vice president Richard M. Nixon drafted the foundation of the Twenty-fifth Amendment when they created letters of agreement between the presidency and the vice presidency in the late 1950s. The letters of agreement detailed the procedures to be followed in case of presidential disability. The following letter was publicized on March 3, 1958. It was used by future administrations, and by the creators of the Twenty-fifth Amendment:

> *(1) In the event of inability the President would—if possible—so inform the Vice President, and the Vice President would serve as Acting President, exercising the powers and duties of the office until the inability had passed.*

> *(2) In the event of an inability which would prevent the President from so communicating with the Vice President, the Vice President, after such consultation as seems to him appropriate under the circumstances, would decide upon the devolution of the powers and duties of the Office and would serve as Acting President until the inability had ended.*

> *(3) The President, in either event, would determine when the inability had ended and at that time would resume the full exercise of the powers and duties of the Office.*

Near the end of his second term, Eisenhower ordered Brownell to explore the possibility of turning the letters of agreement into law or a constitutional amendment. Brownell found that the Constitution did not adequately provide for issues such as 1) the Tyler precedent when a vice president assumed the presidency; 2) how the vice presidency should be filled when vacant; and 3) the procedures to determine and respond to presidential disability. When Congress began considering the Twenty-fifth Amendment in 1963, it used much of Brownell's research.

(1929–1941), and World War II (1941–1945). Even though he suffered many difficult health problems during his terms, the press corps' "splendid deception," as Roosevelt's biographers called it, helped FDR remain in the presidency for an unprecedented four terms.

Presidential recognition of the dangers of presidential disability

Dwight D. Eisenhower was sixty-three years old and had a heart condition when he was elected president of the United States in 1953. In office, Eisenhower suffered three major health problems that threatened his ability to perform his duties of office. On September 23, 1955, he had a kind of heart attack called a coronary thrombosis. He remained hospitalized until November 11. He required surgery on his small intestine in 1956. This affected his workload for nearly a month. On November 25, 1957, he suffered a stroke that affected his speech, and interrupted his normal schedule until December 3.

During each of Eisenhower's recuperation periods, vice president Richard M. Nixon took over his duties. After the first three incidents, Eisenhower became keenly aware that he might not be able to fulfill

The debates around drafting the Twenty-fifth Amendment came soon after the assassination of President John F. Kennedy. Reproduced by permission of Corbis-Bettmann.

his duties as president before the end of his term. Even though he did not personally like Nixon, Eisenhower—with the help of attorney general and close friend Herbert Brownell—drafted agreements with Nixon for use if Eisenhower became disabled. These agreements became the foundation for the future Twenty-fifth Amendment (see sidebar on page 473).

Crafting the Twenty-fifth Amendment

In 1963, the Senate Judiciary Committee began debating issues of presidential succession and disability as a possible amendment to the Constitution. At the time, John F. Kennedy, the youngest president ever to be elected, had recently been killed by Lee Harvey Oswald. Kennedy's successor was the fifty-five year old, chain-smoking Lyndon B. Johnson. He had suffered a severe heart attack in the 1950s, and was rumored to have suffered another upon news of Kennedy's death. Next in line for the presidency were a seventy-four-year old speaker of the house, and an eighty-six-year old president pro tempore of the Senate.

Lyndon B. Johnson was sworn in as president soon after the death of President John F. Kennedy, although the Twenty-fifth Amendment was not yet drafted or ratified. Reproduced by permission of AP/Wide World Photos.

Twenty-fifth Amendment

The American public was openly concerned about the health of the country's leadership.

Senator Estes Kefauver began the debates about presidential succession and disability in the Senate Judiciary Committee. But shortly after he convinced the Committee to begin the process of amending the Constitution, Kefauver died. Senator Birch Bayh took over. Bayh spent the next two years drafting what would become the Twenty-fifth Amendment.

Debates quickly resolved that the Tyler precedent was valid. In case a president does not complete his term of office, the vice president becomes the president. Senators struggled to define rules to fill a vacant vice presidency. Finally, they agreed that the president should nominate a new vice president, and the House and Senate should confirm his decision.

The most difficult task in shaping the Twenty-fifth Amendment was defining the procedures for determining presidential disability. If the president identified his own disability, the procedure would be rather simple. But what if the president did not recognize his own disability? Who would have the authority to pronounce the president incapable of fulfilling his duties?

In the end, the task was given to the vice president, and a majority of the president's cabinet "or of such other body as Congress may by law provide." It was done this way because Congressmen reasoned that those people would best know how well the president was performing in office. The amendment included ways for the president to contest (dispute) the findings, and gave the president the ultimate authority to decide the termination of the presidential disability.

When the amendment passed through Congress on July 6, 1965, state legislatures quickly ratified it. The Twenty-fifth Amendment was ratified by more than the required thirty-eight states by February 10, 1967.

Using the Twenty-Fifth Amendment

The Twenty-fifth Amendment was first invoked after the resignation of a corrupt vice president and president. In 1973, President Richard M. Nixon used the amendment to replace vice president Spiro T. Agnew. Agnew resigned from the vice presidency as part of a deal with federal prosecutors. They had a strong case that indicted (charged) Agnew with bribery and tax evasion. He pled "no contest" to the charges on October

The assassination attempt on President Ronald Reagan left him disabled much longer than his administration let the public know.

Reproduced by permission of AP/Wide World Photos.

THE PRESIDENT IS SHOT

The Twenty-fifth Amendment provided clear instructions for dealing with a circumstance that made the president temporarily unable to perform his duties. Yet these instructions did not consider the reluctance of the president's staff to declare the president disabled.

The American public watched in horror as John Hinkley, Jr. shot several times at Ronald Reagan on March 30, 1981. The president's smile and wave quickly faded as gunshots rang out when he and his entourage (group of associates) emerged from the Hilton Hotel in Washington, D.C. The president, Presidential Press Secretary James Brady, a Secret Service agent, and a local police officer took bullets before Hinkley was pinned to the ground. In less than five minutes, the president was at the hospital. He was operated on within an hour.

A panic raced through the nation, one that had not been felt since President John F. Kennedy was shot in 1963. The White House staff was eager to reassure the public. They decided not to invoke the Twenty-fifth Amendment while Reagan was in the hospital, nor during the time of his recovery—even though the president was unconscious during his surgery, and very weak afterwards. Reagan was nearly back to his regular schedule by June 1981. His doctor, Daniel Ruge, later told author Herbert L. Abrams that Reagan probably had not fully recovered until October. The country had been without a fully functioning leader for quite some time.

White House communications director David Gergen later explained why the Twenty-fifth Amendment was not invoked. "There

10, 1973. On October 12, Nixon nominated the well-liked House Minority Leader Gerald R. Ford to replace Agnew.

With the scandal of his vice president behind him, Nixon soon became embroiled (caught up) in the controversy surrounding the Watergate Affair. On June 17, 1972, there was a burglary of the National Committee at the Watergate apartment complex in Washington, D.C. Investigations into the burglary implicated the Nixon administration. By 1974, Congress had begun impeachment hearings. Nixon resigned on August 9, 1974. Ford assumed the vacant presidency the same day. On August 20, Ford nominated New York Governor Nelson A. Rockefeller for vice

is a very great reluctance to move on the Twenty-fifth. Everyone is hesitant because in effect you are expressing less than full confidence in your chief executive. There is an overwhelming urge to convey a serene view to the world ...," as quoted in *The President Has Been Shot*.

And at the time, Reagan's doctor did not offer any help in deciding whether Reagan was disabled. While Dr. Ruge recalled being prepared to deal with a dead president, he was not prepared for the consequences of a disabled one. As quoted in *The President Has Been Shot*, Dr. Ruge noted that "if [the president] had had an injury like Brady's which made him completely disabled, my role would have been clear. Probing into the relative degrees of competence is another matter." In the end, the greatest concern remained keeping the American public calm, and reassuring them that their president would soon recover.

Several years after this incident, the White House staff and many of the doctors agreed that the Twenty-fifth Amendment should have been invoked. Senator Bayh criticized the administration. In *The President Has Been Shot*, he was quoted as saying, "This was a time for a good precedent to be set. There is a tenacious desire to hold on to presidential power and not to trust other people with it. I think the president botched it."

Reagan did invoke the Twenty-fifth Amendment later, however. In 1985, while having a growth removed from his intestine, Reagan turned the presidency over to Vice President George Bush for seven hours.

president. By December, both houses had confirmed the nomination. For the first time in American history, the leaders of the country had not been elected to their positions by the American people.

Conclusion

The Twenty-fifth Amendment clarifies the process of transferring executive power, and provides guidance for presidential disability. It has also clarified the duties of the vice president, and, in turn, has increased the significance of that office. But the sections addressing presidential dis-

ability continue to trouble some legal scholars and some modern presidential administrations. The amendment spells out how to transfer power when the president is disabled, but does not address an underlying problem with presidential disability: a president's reluctance to reveal weakness.

Historically, presidents have not liked to admit that they can't perform their duties. Since the ratification of the Twenty-fifth Amendment, presidents have invoked it sparingly. Rather than use the amendment for every illness, the president and his entourage carefully consider questions such as: who will run the country if the Twenty-fifth amendment is not invoked? If the vice president takes over for a short time, will he upset the daily routines established by the president? What would happen to the country if the public thought the president was weak? Would the public have the same confidence in the president when he returned from his disability?

These questions highlight the fact that the Twenty-fifth Amendment does not define disability. Each president is free to decide for himself. More recent presidents have continued to search for ways around invoking the Twenty-fifth Amendment. In 1997, President Bill Clinton chose to undergo knee surgery with only a local anesthetic. This way, he could remain conscious and avoid presidential disability.

There are other possible problems concerning presidential disability in addition to the reluctance of presidents to use the amendment in cases of disability. Some legal experts worry about an instance when a president disagrees about a disability with his or her vice president and cabinet. Sections three and four may be so difficult to follow that effective governing would be impeded (blocked). This instance has yet to occur. But by the early twenty-first century, the Twenty-fifth amendment had worked to ensure a more fluid transition of executive power if needed.

For More Information

Books

Abrams, Herbert L. *"The President Has Been Shot": Confusion, Disability, and the Twenty-fifth Amendment in the Aftermath of the Attempted Assassination of Ronald Reagan.* New York: W.W. Norton and Company, 1992.

Bernstein, Richard B., with Jerome Agel. *Amending America: If We Love the Constitution So Much, Why Do We Keep Trying to Change It?* New York: Times Books, 1993.

Feerick, John D. *From Failing Hands, The Story of Presidential Succession.* New York: Fordham University Press, 1965.

Feerick, John D., with foreword by Birch Bayh. *The Twenty-Fifth Amendment: Its Complete History and Earliest Applications.* New York: Fordham University Press, 1992.

Feinberg, Barbara Silberdick. *Constitutional Amendments.* New York: Twenty-First Century Books, 1996.

Levy, Leonard W., Kenneth L. Karst, Dennis J. Mahoney, and John G. West, Jr., eds. *Encyclopedia of the American Constitution.* New York: Macmillan, 1986 and 1992 supp.

Mabie, Margot C. J. *The Constitution: Reflections of a Changing Nation.* New York: Henry Holt Books, 1987.

Palmer, Kris E., editor. *Constitutional Amendments, 1789 to the Present.* Detroit, MI: Gale Group, 2000.

Web Sites

The U.S. Constitution Online. [Online] http:/www.usconstitution.net/constnot.html (accessed August, 2000).

Twenty-sixth Amendment

SECTION 1. The right of the citizens of the United States, who are eighteen years of age or older, to vote shall not be denied or abridged by the United States or by any State on account of age.

SECTION 2. The Congress shall have power to enforce this article by appropriate legislation.

The Twenty-sixth Amendment, which gave anyone over the age of eighteen the right to vote in federal, state, and local elections, was quickly slapped together and ratified in the face of possible contradictions between state and federal voting laws. The amendment was ratified by the states in just 107 days, making it the quickest amendment ever approved by the states. The speed with which it was ratified masked the controversy and legal problems that led to its creation.

The Right to Vote

The question of who may vote has been a primary concern of democracies since their origins in ancient Greece. As the creators of democracy, the Greeks thought citizenship was very important. In fact, the philosopher Aristotle himself argued that the highest calling one had was as a citizen of society. Greek citizens were responsible for contributing to society by fulfilling their duties as teachers, soldiers, merchants, etc. Voting was one of the most important acts of a citizen, but the right to vote was by no means universal. The Greeks eventually decided to give the vote to males over the age of eighteen, while the Romans fixed the minimum voting age for males at twenty–five. Most ancient civilizations required that citizens be property owners, and they excluded women from voting.

Voting requirements have continued to be an issue for modern societies. The Twenty–sixth Amendment to the Constitution was the fourth

RATIFICATION FACTS

PROPOSED: Submitted by Congress to the states on March 23, 1971.

RATIFICATION: Ratified by the required three-fourths of states (38 of 50) on July 1, 1971, and by four more states in November of that year. Declared to be part of the Constitution on July 5, 1971.

RATIFYING STATES: Connecticut, March 23, 1971; Delaware, March 23, 1971; Minnesota, March 23, 1971; Tennessee, March 23, 1971; Washington, March 23, 1971; Hawaii, March 24, 1971; Massachusetts, March 24, 1971; Montana, March 29, 1971; Arkansas, March 30, 1971; Idaho, March 30, 1971; Iowa, March 30, 1971; Nebraska, April 2, 1971; New Jersey, April 3, 1971; Kansas, April 7, 1971; Michigan, April 7, 1971; Alaska, April 8, 1971; Maryland, April 8, 1971; Indiana, April 8, 1971; Maine, April 9, 1971; Vermont, April 16, 1971; Louisiana, April 17, 1971; California, April 19, 1971; Colorado, April 27, 1971; Pennsylvania, April 27, 1971; Texas, April 27, 1971; South Carolina, April 28, 1971; West Virginia, April 28, 1971; New Hampshire, May 13, 1971; Arizona, May 14, 1971; Rhode Island, May 27, 1971; New York, June 2, 1971; Oregon, June 4, 1971; Missouri, June 14, 1971; Wisconsin, June 22, 1971; Illinois, June 29, 1971; Alabama, June 30, 1971; Ohio, June 30, 1971; North Carolina, July 1, 1971; Oklahoma, July 1, 1971.

amendment to clarify voting rights; the others were the Fifteenth, the Nineteenth, and the Twenty–third. Before the Twenty–sixth Amendment was ratified by Congress, however, only citizens aged twenty–one or older were allowed to vote. And during our country's early days, many states restricted voting rights to white male property owners. Women, slaves, and all others who did not fit into this very rigid category were denied the right to vote.

The road to a more inclusive democracy in America tells the story of developing ideas of citizenship. As various colonies required more of their occupants, such as paying taxes, military service, and the like, they were forced to extend suffrage, or the right to vote, to more people. Events like the American Revolution (1775–1783) also influenced changes in voting requirements. People were troubled by the fact that

**Twenty-sixth
Amendment**

they could go to war and die for their country yet still be unable to vote. Slogans like "Old enough to fight, old enough to die"—first used during the Revolutionary period to argue for lowering the voting age—began to resonate with young adults who resented their partial exclusion from the category "citizen." The adoption of a uniform voting age for all states, however, would not come about until the twentieth century.

Wartime Blues

The War of 1812 provided potential voters with another opportunity to argue for an extension of male suffrage. Supporters of a lower minimum voting age argued that those who served in the war fought equally well, regardless of their age. Additionally, many argued that the civic responsibilities of eighteen- and twenty-one-year olds were so similar that to deny the former the right to vote was an outdated formality. Despite the logic of these arguments, however, most states resisted changing the age requirement and opted only for relaxing property ownership requirements attached to voting rights.

The Civil War (1861–1865) revived calls for youth suffrage in the North. With over 500,000 Union soldiers seventeen years old or younger, the time seemed right to argue for a reduction of the minimum age; in fact, one future president, William McKinley, was among those in that age group who fought bravely in the Civil War. Although the reform issue was argued at the New York Constitutional Convention in 1867, it fell flat. Instead, support for changes in suffrage regulations focused primarily on extending the right to vote to black Americans; women and those under the age of twenty-one would have to wait.

WORLD WAR I. America's entrance into World War I (1914–1918) meant that the nation needed a pool of soldiers ready to protect the country's interests overseas. To meet this need, Congress passed the Selective Service Act in 1917. This act declared that those between the ages of twenty-one and thirty could be drafted to fight for America. Realizing that more soldiers might be needed to fight for their country, however, Congress lowered the draft age to eighteen the following year. Although this prompted the push for a change in the voting age, little actual progress was made at this time. Youths frustrated by the hypocrisy they saw in this move asked an age-old question: How could they be mature enough to pick up a machine gun and go to war, yet too immature to cast a ballot at the polls?

Although women were successful in getting the vote with the adoption of the Nineteenth Amendment in 1920, the issue of lowering the age requirement largely disappeared from the public spotlight with the end of World War I. The onset of World War II, though, brought renewed vigor against what many saw as the hypocrisy of the voting age requirement.

THE DRAFT AND WORLD WAR II. With the first peacetime draft issued by Congress in 1940, the question of suffrage reform was once again brought into public discussion. Although polls showed that the vast majority of Americans looked unfavorably upon lowering the voting age (eighty–three percent versus seventeen percent, according to a Gallup poll conducted in 1939 and cited in Kris Palmer's *Constitutional Amendments*), supporters remained determined to sway the majority. The first attempt to pass a constitutional amendment came from Senator Harley Kilgore—a Democrat from West Virginia—before America officially entered World War II in 1941. The growth in the number of youths attending American schools also encouraged those working for voting reform. Such groups as the Young Voter's League, formed in 1941, hoped to organize the huge numbers of potential voters now coming of age.

By this time, there were signs of real progress. Though supporters of a lower voting age did not yet constitute a majority, they were at least becoming more bipartisan. In 1942, Michigan's Republican Senator Arthur Vandenberg, as quoted in *Youth's Battle for the Ballot,* opened his argument to the president with this comment: "Mr. President, if young men are to be drafted at eighteen years of age to fight for their government, they ought to be entitled to vote at eighteen years of age for the kind of government for which they are best satisfied to fight."

Feeling confident that support for an amendment was growing, backers began pushing proposals at both the state and federal levels. Only one of the numerous proposals, however, was successful. In 1943, Georgia became the first state to lower the voting age to eighteen. The irony, of course, was that this progressive move on the part of Georgians came at the same time that their state constitution denied African Americans the right to vote.

Inching Toward a Majority?

The end of World War II signaled a change in the number of Americans willing to consider lowering the voting age. In fact, one poll gave the supporters a majority, though it proved to be short-lived. By the late

THE SELECTIVE SERVICE ACT OF 1917

Throughout most of U.S. history, cash bonuses were paid to enlistees to attract them to military service; this practice was widely known as the "Bounty System." During the French and Indian Wars, the Revolutionary War, the War of 1812, and the Mexican-American War, bonuses included land grants as well as cash incentives; Civil War bonuses were only given in cash. In general, states offered higher bonuses than the federal government. Wealthy areas sometimes offered as much as $1,000 to entice soldiers to their ranks, while federal bonuses were generally in the range of $100 to $400, depending on the length of enlistment.

The bounty system was not without its problems. Abuses were common. Enlistees would simply collect their bonuses and then never show up for actual service. It was not uncommon, in fact, for individuals to go through this process several times in various locations to maximize their profits. Because of such problems, and because World War I demanded a more reliable form of troop mobilization, the practice of handing out bonuses for military service was outlawed in the Selective Service Act of 1917.

The American contribution to World War I, while relatively small compared to that of the Allies, was still considerable in terms of the outcome of the war. The U.S. Navy, fully prepared at the beginning of U.S. entry into the battle, joined the British in overcoming the submarine threat posed by the Germans. Additionally, the U.S. Army was, by this time, some 4 million soldiers strong—due mainly to conscription under the Selective Service Act. The huge infusion of manpower under this Act tipped the balance in the favor of the Allies and helped end the war in November 1918.

The United States first enacted a peacetime draft with the Selective Training and Service Act of 1940. The idea was to train a limited

1940s, support for an amendment seemed to be fading into the background once again. Indeed, it appeared that crises were the only times that support for an amendment could be sustained in the public realm. If times were quiet, people saw no need to make a change.

As it happened, the second half of the twentieth century was full of crises. From the beginning of the Cold War (1945–1991)to the wars in

number of soldiers—no more than 900,000 at any one time—for a fixed period of service that began as one year and was later extended to eighteen months. The U.S. entry into World War II, however, placed a greater demand by the military for new soldiers. Because of this, another Selective Service Act was established that made men between eighteen and forty–five eligible for military service; the act also required all men between eighteen and sixty–five to register. From 1940 to 1947, the government drafted over 10 million men to serve in the military. The end of the war brought another change to the act. The new legislation required men between the ages of eighteen and twenty–six to register, and specified that those between the ages of nineteen and twenty–six could be required to serve for twenty–one months, followed by an additional five years of reserve duty.

The Selective Service Act underwent various other changes with the Korean and Vietnam Wars. It was the Vietnam War, however, that eventually led to its temporary demise. Many young men sought educational deferments, which allowed them to postpone their service if they were enrolled in school, or tried to obtain conscientious objector exemptions from their draft boards. But since these and other kinds of exemptions were given more often to middle-class white men than to working-class and poor men, conscription became a major issue of debate. Demonstrations were held at draft boards and many young men chose to evade the draft altogether for various reasons; many fled the country and some even went to prison. By 1973, social protest led to the abolition of conscription in favor of an all-voluntary military, and President Gerald Ford later granted clemency to many draft dodgers.

The issue of draft registration, however, will simply not die. In 1980, Congress reinstituted registration for men between the ages of eighteen and twenty–five. In the event of a crisis, age and a random lottery would dictate who would be drafted to serve in the military.

Korea (1950–1953) and Vietnam (1954–1975), there was plenty of trouble around which supporters of a voting age amendment could mobilize the call for parity, or equality, between what was expected of the country's youth and what was afforded them in terms of their rights and privileges as citizens. Even McCarthyism—the name given to Senator Joseph McCarthy's campaign in the late 1940s and early 1950s to expose "sup-

posed" Communist spies in the United States—was used to attempt to advance the cause, for if potential Communists were allowed to vote, argued some, the least this country could do was to extend the same opportunity to its patriots.

The time after World War II also brought more prestige to the ranks of suffrage support. Convinced that if the country could ask youngsters to go into battle it should also allow them to vote, President Dwight D. Eisenhower began actively pushing for a national amendment that would lower the voting age; indeed, with the president behind them how could the voting age suffragists fail?

States' Rights

Though supporters of lowering the voting age were gaining support, many failed to see that the issue at hand was larger than a mere lowering of the voting age. Since this country's founding, the debate over the right of states to set their own laws, rather than having them forced upon them by the federal government, has been intense. The resistance to voting reform

Many felt that if young men were old enough to fight in wars, then they were old enough to vote. Courtesy of the Library of Congress.

on the grounds of immaturity, for example, was significant. Perhaps more pervasive, however, was the resistance among state lawmakers to allowed the federal government to infringe upon the rights of states to set their own suffrage terms. In this sense, then, young people were being used as the battlefield upon which a larger war was being fought.

Opposition to the voting age amendment was particularly strong in the South, where resentment over federal intrusion into state politics has a long history. This resentment, traceable to at least Civil War times, was very clear when, in 1954, lawmakers failed by a vote of thirty–four to twenty–four to pass a resolution lowering the voting age. Feeling intense pressure to end their blockage of voting rights for blacks, Southern states were in no mood to respond positively to federal pressure aimed at lowering the voting age as well. The only exception to this came in Kentucky when, in 1954, the General Assembly became the second state to lower the voting age to eighteen.

By midcentury, however, even the prestige of presidential support was not enough to convince the vast majority of Americans and lawmakers that supporting a lower voting age was in America's interest. The battle continued, though quietly, on the state front for another decade. On the federal level, not much progress was made despite Eisenhower's call for a federal amendment in his 1956 State of the Union address. In the end, it took another major crisis to bring the debate back into the public domain.

The Vietnam War

The Vietnam War was the event that finally tipped the scales in favor of a federal amendment lowering the voting age. Upset by U.S. participation in the war, young Americans began holding protests during the 1960s. Not only did they protest the war itself, but many revived the slogan, "If we're old enough to fight, we're old enough to vote," and added it to their list of complaints surrounding U.S. involvement in Vietnam. Indeed, their logic was sound. If those under twenty–one were old enough to be drafted by the government to fight in a war that might cost them their lives, it only followed that they should at least have a voice in the affairs of the government and in the broader political process. Moreover, eighteen-year-olds were no longer protected under juvenile laws and had to bear the criminal and civil consequences of their actions. Because of this, they argued, they were already legally adults who should be afforded all of the benefits that came with their new responsibilities.

**Twenty-sixth
Amendment**

Some older Americans, of course, continued to argue against handing the vote to those under twenty–one. Their arguments focused primarily on the notion that young people had no real stake in the political process of the country and their participation in it would lead to political instability. Furthermore, they argued that most people between twenty–one and thirty never voted anyway, so it would be foolish to assume that those under twenty–one would be any different. Although it might have been true that many younger Americans did not vote as regularly as their elders did, to deny those who would take the vote seriously the opportunity to participate on those grounds was, at best, weak logic.

Protestors picked up on the weakness of such arguments and countered with stronger arguments of their own. Chief among their points was the draft, which gave them a stake in their country. Additionally, sixty percent of eighteen- to twenty-year-olds at this time worked and paid taxes. What's more, this age group had a high level of education compared to many of their parents, who did not attend college—a fact that further strengthened the legitimacy of age-based suffrage reform.

Many young Americans protested the war in Vietnam, both because they disagreed with the United States' participation, and because they felt they were not being extended rights that were due to them.

Indeed, many of the arguments against lowering the voting age began to crumble under the weight of changing times. No longer could older Americans argue that the youth were uninformed and therefore a threat to the stability of the political process. In fact, because of the emerging mass media during the 1960s, young Americans were much better informed than their counterparts were years before. Not only did the media and public opinion play a direct role in ending the Vietnam War, but they also played a significant role in suffrage reform. The hypocrisy of denying youth the right to vote was no longer easy to ignore. Young people had demonstrated political responsibility by participating in service organizations and political campaigns. Perhaps what the older generation feared most was the challenge to the status quo posed by young voters.

Supporters of these young Americans argued that their enthusiasm for participating in the political process should be acknowledged and rewarded. Furthermore, if their enthusiasm was harnessed at a young age there was a better chance of nourishing life-long participators in the political process. Although these arguments and the protests that arose out of the Vietnam War added significant momentum to the fight for suffrage reform, it would still be several years before the dream of a federal amendment to the Constitution would be realized.

The Final Stretch

In 1965, Congress passed the Voting Rights Act, which once again brought the issue of voting age before politicians. Although the purpose of the act was to make it easier for African Americans to vote by eliminating literacy tests and authorizing the attorney general to send federal examiners to register black voters under certain circumstances, the issue of voting age came into play when the Voting Rights Act was amended in 1970. Backed by the momentum of the Civil Rights movement and by the Voting Rights Act, supporters of voting age reform began lobbying their representatives to bring a federal amendment before Congress once again. Their pressure worked. Many politicians began to support lowering the voting age. The final seal of approval came when the Nixon Administration backed the idea of an amendment.

The battle, however, was not yet over. Rather than pushing through an amendment, the Senate instead passed legislation aimed at altering the voting age. The Voting Rights Act of 1970 was a practical law because lawmakers felt that an amendment had little chance of surviving the approval process in the Judiciary Committee, where one of its longtime

Many politicians have started to target the young vote for major elections. Al Gore appeared on MTV while campaigning for president in 2000. Reproduced by permission of AP/Wide World Photos.

members, Emanuel Celler, was strongly in opposition. Much to their surprise, however, Celler was no obstacle to the passage of the legislation and on June 22, 1970, Nixon signed the law into effect.

Yet the legislation had one major problem: it contradicted the Constitution. States complained that the federal government could not set their voting requirements; the federal government argued that it had the authority to prevent states from denying the vote to anyone under the Equal Protection Clause of the Fourteenth Amendment. The Supreme Court reviewed the issue in the case of *Oregon vs. Mitchell* and ruled that that part of the legislation was indeed unconstitutional because the federal government could not set voting requirements for state and local elections. That power was given to individual states in Article I, section 2 of the Constitution and many states resisted what they saw as an infringement on their turf by the federal government. The federal government could, however, according to Article I, Section 4; Article II, Section 1; and the Necessary and Proper Clause of the Constitution, lower the voting age for national elections.

And this is exactly what it did. The minimum voting age for national elections would be eighteen, and each state would be left to determine their own minimums. For obvious reasons, this system would never have worked; chaos and confusion would have ruled at the polling booths across the country. Not only would the expense of holding separate elections on the state and federal levels have been considerable, but maintaining two sets of voter registration books would have made the whole process quite cumbersome. Not surprisingly, the prospect of this confusion and added expense played into the hands of the supporters of suffrage reform. States quickly, if in some cases reluctantly, backed a federal amendment lowering the voting age before Congress could enact the confusing legislation.

The result was the proposal and quick ratification of the Twenty–sixth Amendment to the Constitution, despite the fact that roughly two–thirds of the country was still against the idea of eighteen-year-olds voting. Ironically, on one level the amendment was only ratified to avoid a messy situation. The victory for the supporters of the amendment, however, was real; they could now fully participate in the political process and enjoy the benefits of voting, which is so closely tied to our definition of citizenship.

Twenty-sixth Amendment

For More Information

Books

Anastaplo, George. *The Amendments to the Constitution.* Baltimore: Johns Hopkins University Press, 1995.

Bernstein, Richard B., with Jerome Agel. *Amending America: If We Love the Constitution So Much, Why Do We Keep Trying to Change It?* New York: Times Books, 1993.

Cultice, Wendell W. *Youth's Battle for the Ballot.* Westport, Connecticut: Greenwood Press, 1992.

Feinberg, Barbara S. *The Amendments.* New York: Henry Holt, 1996.

Morin, Isobel V. *Our Changing Constitution: How and Why We Have Amended It.* Brookfield, Connecticut: Millbrook Press, 1998.

Palmer, Kris E., editor. *Constitutional Amendments, 1789 to the Present.* Detroit: Gale Group, 2000.

West's Encyclopedia of American Law. 12 vols. St. Paul, MN: West Group, 1998.

Youth Vote: The Registration and Voting Patterns of Youth since the Passage of the 26th Amendment in 1921.. Cleveland: League of Women Voters of Cleveland Educational Fund, 1999.

Web Sites

"The Home Front." [Online] http://jefferson.village.virginia.edu/ seminar/unti10/home.html (accessed 26 June 2000).

"Selective Service." [Online] http://infoplease.kids.lycos.com/ce6/ history/A0844347.html (accessed 26 June 2000).

"The Twenty Sixth Amendment to the Constitution of the United States." [Online] http://nova.acomp.usf.edu/~mhagood/26th1.html (accessed 25 June 2000).

"U.S. Constitution: Twenty-Sixth Amendment." [Online] http:// supreme.findlaw.com/Constitution/amendment 26/ (Accessed 25 June 2000).

Twenty-seventh Amendment

No law, varying the compensation for the services of Senators and Representatives, shall take effect, until an election of Representatives shall have intervened.

The Twenty–seventh Amendment places a control on Congress' power to raise the wages of its own members. As the legislative body of the United States, Congress does make the laws which set the salaries of senators and representatives. To prevent Congress from misusing this power, the Twenty–seventh Amendment states that any law that Congress passes to raise the pay of members of Congress will only become law after the next election of the House of Representatives.

This delay gives citizens a chance to vote for or against the representatives who passed the Congressional pay raise, before those representatives can benefit from the raise. Members of the House of Representatives serve a two year term, so an election of Representatives will occur relatively soon after any pay raise is passed into law. Members of the Senate serve for six years, so Senators do sometimes benefit from pay raises that were passed during their term. However, there are only one hundred senators, two from each state, while there are 435 representatives in the House. Therefore, the majority of members of Congress will be held responsible in an election before they can benefit from any pay raise that is passed during their term of office.

The Twenty–seventh Amendment is unique among the constitutional amendments, because the ratification process took 203 years to complete. When the Twenty–seventh Amendment was first proposed in 1789, by Virginia statesman James Madison, it was meant to be the Second Amendment. However, it did not gain enough support at that time for ratification. Over the next two centuries only two other states ratified the

Twenty-seventh Amendment

amendment; a campaign in the 1980s led to ratification by thirty two more states, and the amendment finally became law.

The Question of Paying Congress

The subject of who should pay representatives to the national legislature was the topic of long debate at the 1787 Constitutional Convention in Philadelphia. Anti-Federalists at the convention favored strong state governments where most of the political power rested with the states. Some anti-Federalist delegates like Oliver Ellsworth of Connecticut and Hugh Williamson of North Carolina proposed that state governments should pay their own national representatives, and the individual state legislatures could then decide how much to pay their Congresspeople.

The Federalists, who favored a strong central government, argued against this idea. Led by such backers of strong federal power as Virginians James Madison and George Mason, the Federalists insisted that having the separate states pay their own representatives would be a bad idea. For one thing, it would make the representatives almost completely independent of the federal government, and that would weaken the central structure of the country. For another thing, wealthy states would be able to pay their Congresspeople much more than smaller, poorer states, and this would create an unfair imbalance among the members of Congress.

During the Continental Congresses (First Continental Congress, 1774–76; Second Continental Congress, 1778–79), individual colonies had paid their own representatives. Since the colonial treasuries had often been unstable, the result had been that many delegates had been paid irregularly or not at all. Madison pointed this out, saying that if legislators were not paid regularly and fairly well then many people might not be interested in the job. Only those who could afford to accept low salaries would run for Congress. Elbridge Gerry, the delegate from Massachusetts, said "It would seem to be a maxim of democracy to starve the public servants," according to *Constitutional Amendments: 1789 to the Present.*

This brought up another topic of argument—if Congressmen were to be paid by the federal government, who would decide how much they would be paid? Many delegates felt it would be dangerous to allow members of Congress to set their own salaries; it would be too easy for them to pay themselves too much. Madison's suggestion was that the wages should be set by comparing them to some standard cost, like the price of wheat. Other delegates, such as Gouverneur Morris of Pennsylvania, felt that the members of Congress could be trusted to make the laws which set their rate of pay.

After lengthy debate, the delegates finally hammered out the language of Article 1, Section 6, Clause 1, the Compensation Clause of the United States Constitution: "The Senators and Representatives shall receive a Compensation for their services, to be ascertained by Law, and paid out by the Treasury of the United States." The first salary set by Congress in 1789 for representatives and senators was six dollars per day.

The Long History of "Madison's Amendment"

Shortly after the Constitution was ratified in 1789, James Madison proposed a list of amendments to the new document. The second of these

JAMES MADISON (1751–1836)

Born into a family of wealthy plantation owners in Port Conway, Virginia, James Madison was a sickly child who developed a lifelong love of books and learning. In his youth he learned to read Greek, Latin, and Spanish as well as English, and, in 1771, he graduated from the College of New Jersey (now Princeton University) after studying philosophy and theology. Madison was also a scholar of government and politics, and his knowledge in these areas made him an important figure in the early history of the United States. In 1776, Madison was elected to the Virginia Constitutional Convention, where he helped create the government of that state. In 1780, he became the youngest member of the Continental Congress in Philadelphia, where he served from 1780 to 1783 and in 1787. From 1784 to 86 he served as a representative in the Virginia state legislature.

A set of rules called the Articles of Confederation had been drawn up in 1776 (and ratified in 1781) to help the new states unite into a nation, but these articles provided the federal government with so little power that they made governing difficult. James Madison joined New York lawyer and politician Alexander Hamilton to call for a convention to frame a new constitution, one with a more powerful central government. The result was the Constitutional Convention, which met in Philadelphia in 1787.

James Madison contributed so much of his knowledge and leadership in the formation of the Constitution that he is often called the "Father" or "Master Builder" of the Constitution. After the Constitution was written, Madison, along with Hamilton and another New York lawyer and statesman, John Jay, wrote dozens of letters to newspapers under the name "Publius" to try to convince Americans to ratify the new government. After the Constitution was ratified in 1789, Madison wrote a list of twelve amendments to the new Constitution. These were pre-

amendments, intended to place a limit on Congress' ability to set its own salaries, read, "No law, varying the compensation for the services of Senators and Representatives, shall take effect, until an election of Representatives shall have intervened." Madison included this amendment because a variety of citizens, mostly in letters to newspapers, had raised fears that Congress had too much power by being able to set their own salaries.

sented to Congress and ten were eventually ratified and made into law as the Bill of Rights.

Madison continued to serve the new government as a representative to Congress from the state of Virginia from 1789 to 1797. In 1801 he went to work for the executive branch of the government as secretary of state for his close friend and fellow Virginian, Thomas Jefferson. Madison served as secretary of state under Jefferson for two terms, then, in 1808 was himself elected to be the fourth president of the United States.

Madison was more skillful as a political scholar than as a leader and his presidency is best remembered for the mistakes he made that led to the War of 1812, sometimes called the "Second War of Independence." Madison, determined to stop British attacks on American ships at sea, placed an embargo on the British. This meant that British ships could not enter American ports or sell their goods in the United States. The British fought back, and war was declared. The young United States was not prepared for war, and the war was not a popular one. Business owners, angry because the war was costing them money called it "Mr. Madison's War." The worst point for the United States came in 1814, when the British overran Washington, D.C., and burned the White House, forcing the Madisons to flee to Virginia. However, the war ended shortly thereafter, with many compromises on both sides, and Madison's popularity as a president increased as the country became more prosperous, partly as a result of new trading arrangements with Britain that came out of the war.

After his second term as president, Madison retired from public life to his estate in Montpelier, Virginia. He was much respected by the citizens of his time as one of those who helped create their new nation. Madison was a productive writer and nine volumes of his papers and writings were collected by Gaillard Hunt in 1900 and published as *The Writings of James Madison, His Public Papers and His Private Correspondence.*

By 1791, when the first ten amendments to the new Constitution (commonly called the Bill of Rights) were ratified, only six states had approved the amendment about changes in Congressional salaries. These were Maryland, North Carolina, South Carolina, Delaware, Vermont, and Virginia.

**Twenty-seventh
Amendment**

"Madison's Amendment," as it came to be called, disappeared from public view for many years. Though the amendment contained no time limit for ratification in its wording, most people believed that the amendment had failed. However, the subject of how much Congress paid its own members continued to arouse both interest and suspicion among citizens, and, occasionally, both politicians and voters remembered James Madison's amendment.

PAYING CONGRESS IN THE NINETEENTH CENTURY. The next major change in Congressional salaries occurred in 1817, when Congress voted not only to raise salaries, but to change its payment method from a daily sum ("per diem") to a yearly salary. Many citizens

In 1873 when the "Salary Grab Act" was passed, it was really just a version of the "Madison Amendment," drafted by James Madison in 1789. Courtesy of the Library of Congress.

were against this change and the public outcry caused Congress to repeal the new salary law. During the next election, angry voters rejected many of the Congressmen who had voted for the increase, and Congress did not attempt another salary change for forty years.

In 1855, Congress did switch to a yearly salary, and in 1866 salaries were raised by sixty-six percent. There was little opposition to those moves, and only seven years later, in 1873, Congress passed a law raising its salaries once more. Enraged citizens called the 1873 law the "Salary Grab Act," and it not only raised Congressional wages by another fifty percent per year, but also made the raise retroactive to 1872, which meant that Congress would receive the higher pay for the previous year of their service as well. Voter opposition to the higher salary was so great that many members of Congress returned their raises.

In 1873, in response to the Salary Grab Act, the state of Ohio retrieved and ratified Madison's congressional salary amendment. There was considerable interest in such an amendment, and other amendments were proposed to limit Congress' powers to raise its pay, but the issue was eventually dropped again. These actions did influence Congress, however, and in 1874 it repealed the 1873 increase and did not attempt to raise wages again for another thirty years.

DEVELOPMENTS IN THE 1900s. Congress would not receive the fifty percent wage increase it had passed in 1873 until 1907, when legislators voted to raise their salaries to $7500 per year. Another increase, passed in the prosperous 1920s, brought salaries to $10,000 per year in 1925. However, the economic hardship of the Great Depression in the 1930s caused Congress to make an unexpected move—to lower Congressional salaries. By 1933, salaries of legislators were back down to $8500 per year.

Salaries of Congresspeople did not continue to go down, however, and the legislature developed methods for avoiding public disapproval as it went about the business of raising its members' pay. Congress set up first the Commission of Judicial and Congressional Salaries in 1953, then the President's Commission of Executive, Legislative, and Judicial Salaries in 1967. The purpose of these boards was to recommend salary raises for government officials. In this way it could appear to voters that an independent commission was responsible for raising legislative salaries, preventing voters from becoming too angry with Congress.

In 1978, however, another Congressional pay raise caught the attention of the state legislators of Wyoming. Once more, they looked to Madison's forgotten amendment to solve the problem. Because the amendment contained no time limit on its ratification, the Wyoming legislature, like the Ohio legislature before it, insisted that it was still a valid amendment. In order to send a message to the United States Congress that unreasonable pay raises would not be tolerated, the Wyoming legislature voted in 1978 to ratify the amendment, becoming the eighth state to do so.

A VERY EFFECTIVE TERM PAPER. What happened next is a clear example of how an individual can cause change in a democratic political system. In 1982, Gregory Watson, a thirty-year-old student at the University of Texas at Austin, wrote a paper for his government class. As his subject, he chose Madison's forgotten amendment. Watson argued that the

Twenty-seventh Amendment

amendment raised an issue that was still important, and that since there was no time limit placed on its ratification, Madison's Amendment could (and should) still be passed into law.

Watson's professor did not agree with his argument and gave him a "C" on his term paper. However, a low grade did not stop Watson from pursuing his interest in the amendment about Congressional pay raises. He began a campaign to revive Madison's Amendment and make it the Twenty–seventh Amendment to the Constitution. To do this, he wrote letters and called representatives in state legislatures around the country, encouraging them to begin the process to ratify the amendment in their state.

Watson's efforts paid off. In 1983, Maine voted to ratify the new amendment, joined in 1984 by Colorado. Other states followed quickly, and, by 1992, forty states had approved the Twenty–seventh Amendment, two more than the thirty–eight required for ratification.

An Atmosphere of Mistrust

While Gregory Watson's political work on behalf of the Twenty–seventh Amendment is an inspiring example of citizen activism, his work alone does not account for the quick passage of a 203-year-old amendment. Another important factor was a general lack of confidence in the ethical values of Congress. In the late 1980s and early 1990s many citizens no longer trusted members of Congress to act fairly and honestly. According to Ruth Ann Strickland in her article in the December 1993, issue of *PS: Political Science & Politics,* a Gallup poll reported that in 1989 only thirty–two percent of American citizens trusted Congress. By the 1991 Gallup poll, that number had gone down to eighteen percent—only eighteen percent of Americans polled trusted the legislative body of their government!

This mistrust was partly due to a series of scandals in Congress that had become public in the 1980s and 1990s. News reports had revealed behavior on the part of senators and representatives that appeared to the public to be abuses of power and privilege. For example, members of Congress had access to free postage for large mailings to voters in their districts, and many abused this privilege to send out frequent mailings to advance their own careers. Unlike average citizens, members of Congress were not charged a fee for writing checks when they did not have the money in the bank account to cover the

Senator Robert C. Byrd of West Virginia was an opponent of the Twenty-seventh Amendment.

Reproduced by permission of AP/Wide World Photos.

check, and many members of Congress abused this privilege by writing many checks they knew would not be covered. Large retirement pensions, free health insurance, free parking, even free haircuts in the Congressional barber shop, all became topics of angry comment.

Adding to this atmosphere of mistrust, Congress proposed a large raise in pay for its members in 1989. This fifty-one percent in crease would have raised annual Congressional salaries from $89,000 to $135,000. Many citizens were outraged, pointing out that the original salary of $89,000 put members of Congress among the wealthiest one percent of U.S. wage earners. Concerned activists like Connecticut lawyer Ralph Nader led the protest, forming groups like the Congressional Accountability Project, Citizens Against Government Waste, the National Taxpayers' Union, and Citizens for a Sound Economy, to fight what they saw as Congressional abuses of power. These groups, along with the general attitude revealed by the Gallup polls, caused Congress to lower their proposed salary raise. However, by 1991, members of the House of Representatives were earning $125,000, and members of the Senate were earning $101,900. These substantial raises, which Congress gave to itself, helped ease the ratification of the Twenty–seventh Amendment. Voters were eager to support a law that would place some controls on Congress' ability to raise its members' salaries.

Twenty-seventh Amendment

RALPH NADER (1934–)

Ralph Nader was born and raised in Winstead, Connecticut, the son of Lebanese immigrants. He graduated from Princeton University in 1955 and got his law degree from Harvard in 1958. While he was in law school, Nader studied lawsuits that arose from automobile injuries, and he became interested in unsafe automobile designs. After working as a lawyer in Connecticut, he moved to Washington, D.C., in 1963 and got a job with the U.S. Department of Labor. In 1965, he published his first famous book, *Unsafe at Any Speed,* an investigation of the U.S. automobile industry. In *Unsafe at Any Speed,* Nader showed how automobile manufacturers themselves were responsible for many auto accidents because they did not have high enough safety standards and did not spend enough of their profits researching how to make cars safer.

This was the beginning of Ralph Nader's long career in consumer protection. Consumer protection means making sure that businesses treat their customers fairly and provide goods and services that are safe and reliable. Nader's research about automobile safety led directly to the passage in 1966 of the National Traffic and Motor Vehicle Safety Act, which gave the government the power to set safety standards for all vehicles sold in the U.S. He then turned his attention to other consumer issues. Working with a team of committed lawyers, who soon came to be called "Nader's Raiders," he published dozens of studies, calling for government regulation of a wide range of consumer products and services. These included baby food, insecticide, mercury poisoning, banking and many more.

The work of Nader and his associates led to the creation of many concerned consumer groups, including Public Citizen, Commercial Alert, the Center for Auto Safety, the National Insurance Consumer Organization and the Health Research Organization. Most of these groups work the same way Nader did when he published *Unsafe at Any Speed:* first investigating to find the facts and publishing reports about them; then

Do Proposed Amendments Live Forever?

It is not uncommon for amendments to the Constitution to be proposed without including a time limit. In fact, in 1921, a man named J. J. Dillon challenged his arrest for importing liquor by stating that the Eighteenth

bringing lawsuits against those who use unfair or unsafe practices; and finally putting pressure on members of Congress to make laws against those practices.

Along with working to protect the rights of consumers, Ralph Nader has also worked hard to protect the rights of citizens. Through such groups as Congress Watch, the Center for Responsive Law, and the Congressional Accountability Project, Nader has encouraged citizens to educate themselves about political issues and participate in their government.

Nader ran for president of the United States in 1996 and again in 2000. Nader did not really expect to become president, but he ran because he felt there was little real difference between the Democratic and Republican parties. Nader felt that by voting for him, citizens could express their dissatisfaction with the two major parties. Nader received 700,000 votes in 1996, even though he only campaigned a fraction as much as the two major candidates, Democrat Bill Clinton and Republican Robert Dole. Nader's candidacy in the extraordinarily close 2000 election, according to many analysts, was an even more significant factor than it had been in the preceding election.

Some people do not approve of Nader's work for the rights of consumers, and others do not agree with his politics, but most do agree that Ralph Nader is honest and sincere in his commitment to social justice and fair business practices. Though *Life* magazine named him one of the 100 most influential people of the twentieth century, Nader has not adopted a celebrity lifestyle, and is almost as famous for his simple life as for his political work. He continues to live in a tiny apartment in the town where he grew up and does not own a car or use a computer. Still, Nader believes that the work of one simple man can have a big effect. "Every major movement for social justice in this country," he says, "started with a handful of people," according to *Mother Jones* writer Ken Silverstein.

Amendment, which made importing liquor illegal, was not a valid amendment. It was not valid, Dillon argued, because it *did* include a time limit on its ratification, and the Constitution did not authorize time limits. Dillon did not win his case. The Supreme Court ruled that Congress had the right to place a time limit on an amendment.

Twenty-seventh Amendment

Still, lawyers, politicians, and legal scholars have continued to argue about the Twenty–seventh Amendment. Did those who wrote the Constitution really intend for an amendment to remain open to ratification for hundreds of years? Many members of Congress felt that the amendment was too old and should not have continued to be valid. Most members of Congress were unwilling to speak out against an amendment controlling Congress' ability to raise salaries, however, because it was a very popular amendment among voters. Voters might see opposition to the amendment as simply the legislators' desire for more money.

Constitutional law professors like Dick Howard of the University of Virginia and Norma Ornstein of the American Enterprise Institute have argued that the amendment was not "timely." That is, the first six ratifications were so old that they no longer reflect what the people in those states think now. Others, including Hamilton Fish, Congressional Representative of New York in 1993, said that the fact that so many states ratified the amendment in the 1980s proved that the amendment is still a timely one. In fact, Laurence Tribe, a law professor at Harvard University, has argued that the Twenty–seventh Amendment's long history makes it even more legitimate, because voters across two centuries have agreed that it is an important law.

For More Information

Books

Bernstein, Richard B., with Jerome Agel. *Amending America: If We Love the Constitution So Much, Why Do We Keep Trying to Change It?* New York: Times Books, 1993.

Celsi, Teresa Noel. *Ralph Nader: The Consumer Revolution.* Brookfield, Connecticut: Millbrook Press, 1991.

Kyvig, David E. *Explicit and Authentic Acts: Amending the U.S. Constitution, 1776-1995.* Lawrence: University of Press of Kansas, 1996.

Palmer, Kris E., editor. *Constitutional Amendments, 1789 to the Present.* Detroit: Gale Group, 2000.

Articles

Clift, Eleanor. "The Tea-Bag Revolution: A Backlash Over the Congressional Pay Raise,"*Newsweek,* February 6, 1989.

DeBenedictis, Don J. "Twenty–seventh Amendment Ratified: Congressional Vote Ends Debate Over 203-Year-Old Pay-Raise Proposal." *American Bar Association Journal 78,* August 1992.

Friedrich, Otto. "How the Deed Was Done: When 55 Men Spent a Hot Summer Arguing Their Way to Greatness," *Time,* July 6, 1987.

"James Madison." *Benet's Reader's Encyclopedia of American Literature, Edition 1.* George Perkins, Barbara Perkins, and Phillip Leininger, editors. New York: HarperCollins, 1991.

Keating, Peter. "Congress Costs You $2.8 Billion Despite 'Reforms.'" *Money,* November 1994.

"The Man Who Would Not Quit." *People,* June 1, 1992.

McCoy, Drew R. "James Madison: 4th U.S. President." *The Reader's Companion to American History, Edition 1991.* Eric Foner and John A. Garraty, editors. Boston : Houghton-Mifflin, 1991.

Michaelis, Laura. "1789 Pay Raise Amendment Returns to Haunt Congress." *Congressional Quarterly Weekly Report,* Vol. 50, No. 19, May 9, 1992.

Murray, Frank J. "Giving Voice to Madison's Words: A Long-Lost Amendment by James Madison is Four States Shy of Ratification." *Insight on the News,* July 16, 1990.

Sifry, Micah L. "Public Citizen No.1." *The Nation,* December, 20, 1999.

Silverstein, Ken. "Candidate Nader—He May Be the Most Intensely Private Man Ever to Seek Public Office. What Makes Ralph Run?" *Mother Jones,* July 2000.

Strickland, Ruth Ann. "The Twenty–seventh Amendment and Constitutional Change by Stealth." *PS: Political Science & Politics,* Vol. 26, No. 4, December, 1993.

Wasserman, Harvey. "Ralph Nader: Consumer Advocate and Activist." *The Reader's Companion to American History, Edition 1991.* Eric Foner and John A. Garraty, editors. Boston : Houghton-Mifflin, 1991.

Twenty-seventh Amendment

Amendment Proposals

The framers of the Constitution deliberately made the process of adding amendments quite difficult. As outlined in Article V, an amendment to the Constitution requires approval by two–thirds of both houses of Congress and three–fourths of the states. Despite the obstacles to passing amendments, over the course of more than 200 years twenty-seven amendments have been added to the Constitution. These twenty-seven amendments all resulted from a widely-shared belief that constitutional change was the best method available to address an issue or solve a problem that the original Constitution did not anticipate. No amendment has ever been passed that served the demands of a minority or even a small majority; in fact, every amendment enjoyed widespread public support at the time of its passage.

For every amendment that has passed and been made a part of the law of the land, there are nearly 500 that have been proposed to Congress. Over the course of American history, some 11,000 amendments have been introduced to Congress. Some have related to weighty matters, such as slavery, equal rights for women, and rights for children; others, such as an amendment calling for renaming the country the "United States of the Earth," have been rather silly. Of all these amendments, only thirty–three have passed Congress and been sent to the states for ratification. And of these, six have never been ratified by the states.

The amendments proposed to the states but not ratified and those that never passed Congress still have a great deal to teach us about the process of amending the Constitution. A number of strong proposals, such as those for a balanced budget amendment or an equal rights amendment, enjoyed substantial support from the public and its representatives and yet have not been ratified. Other proposed amendments have been championed by a minority looking to seek political gain. Whether proposed amendments are serious or silly, they represent an effort by some Americans to reshape the Constitution, the ruling document of the United States.

The Forgotten First Amendment

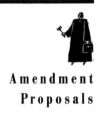

Americans are rightly proud of the Bill of Rights, the name given to the first ten amendments to the Constitution, which were ratified as a group on December 15, 1791. But few know that there were actually twelve potential amendments presented to Congress in 1789. The second of these, concerning congressional pay raises, was eventually ratified and in 1992 became the Twenty–seventh Amendment. But the first, which concerned the size of Congress and the ratio between representatives and population, has never been ratified by the states.

Though ten of the twelve articles proposed to the states (and later ratified as the first ten amendments) pertained to individual rights, Article I spelled out the number of representatives that would represent the people in Congress. Article I stated:

> **After the first enumeration [count] required by the first article of the Constitution, there shall be one Representative for every thirty thousand, until the number shall amount to one hundred, after which the proportion shall be so regulated by Congress, that there shall be not less than one hundred Representatives, nor less than one Representative for every forty thousand persons, until the number of Representatives shall amount to two hundred; after which the proportion shall be so regulated by Congress, that there shall be not less than two hundred Representatives, nor more than one Representative for every fifty thousand persons.**

Under this proposal, the House of Representatives would have grown continually with the growth of the population. Ten states ratified this proposed amendment, one shy of the eleven needed for ratification. But if it had passed, by the late 1990s the House would have had 5,000 members! In fact, legislation passed in 1911 set the size of the House at 435 members, which means that each representative now represents over 500,000 citizens. Historians now view this proposed amendment as a reminder of how poorly early Americans anticipated the future growth of their country.

No Nobles in Government

Early Americans had long been suspicious of so-called "titles of nobility," a granting of special status given by a king or prince. Having left

Amendment Proposals

countries where people with such titles as Lord, Baron, or Count received special privileges and power, Americans wanted to make sure that power in the United States was granted only by the vote of the people. Article I, Section 9, Clause 8 of the Constitution already declared that: "No Title of Nobility shall be granted by the United States; And no Person holding any Office of Profit or Trust under them, shall, without the Consent of the Congress, accept any present, Emolument, Office, or Title, of any kind whatever, from any King, Prince, or foreign State." The framers wanted to be sure that elected representatives could not be influenced by titles or special privileges offered by a foreign power. But

One proposed amendment stated that no citizen of the United States could accept a title of nobility, such as lady, lord, princess, or prince. Reproduced by permission of Archive Photos, Inc.

there were some who felt that the restrictions on titles of nobility should be even stricter.

In January 1810 Senator Philip Reed of Maryland offered the following amendment to the Constitution:

> **If any citizen of the United States shall accept, claim, receive or retain any title of nobility or honour, or shall, without the consent on Congress, accept and retain any present, pension, office or emolument of any kind whatever, from any emperor, king, prince or foreign power, such person shall cease to be a citizen of the United States, and shall**

be incapable of holding any office of trust or profit under them, or either of them.

In plain language, any citizen who accepted any title of nobility would be stripped of his or her U.S. citizenship and forever forbidden from holding public office. The proposed amendment passed the House by a vote of eighty–seven to three and the Senate by a vote of nineteen to five. Though twelve states quickly ratified the amendment, no additional states ever voted for its ratification. (With no time limit on ratification, the amendment could potentially still be passed today.)

MYSTERIOUS MOTIVATIONS. The motivations behind this proposed amendment remain shrouded in mystery. Historians are simply not sure why the proposal appeared at this time and was so quickly passed by Congress. Though there was no recorded debate when the proposal appeared before Congress, historians point to several factors they believe fueled interest in the idea of such an amendment. First, in the years leading up to the War of 1812 (between the United States and England), Americans became increasingly suspicious that both Britain and France were trying to influence American policy. One rumor held that French dictator Napoleon Bonaparte's nephew, who was an American citizen, might try to establish an American monarchy; another rumor suggested that Federalist politicians sided with the British because they hoped to earn titles of nobility. Politicians from both parties were quick to vote for any measure that distanced them from such rumors.

This amendment proposal earned the nickname "the phantom amendment" when a printer's error included the proposed amendment in an 1815 printing of the Constitution. Historians believe that the printer mistakenly believed that South Carolina had ratified the amendment and made it part of the Constitution. In 1874 Congress made most of the provisions of this proposed amendment into a law that applied to U.S. diplomats.

"The Session of Amendments"

By 1860 differences among slave-holding Southern states and free Northern states had reached a fever pitch, and the election of Republican Abraham Lincoln as president proved to many in the South that there was no longer any way to compromise with the North over the issue of slavery. The South wanted to keep slaves, and wanted slavery to be legal in new territories; the North wanted to stop the spread of slavery. When the Thirty–sixth Congress met for its second session shortly after the

Amendment Proposals

presidential election, its members felt that they had one last chance to save the Union. In a session that historian Herman V. Ames called "the session of amendments," Congress heard over two hundred proposals for constitutional amendments designed to save the Union.

The road to disunion had been paved with over half a century of argument and several earlier attempts at constitutional amendments. In 1805 and 1806 several Northern states had called for amendments to stop the trade in slavery, but Congress made such an amendment unnecessary when it passed a law banning the importing of slaves. Though Congress entertained several amendments to ban slavery during the coming decades, the growing sectional conflict was generally handled by compromise legislation. The Missouri Compromise and the Compromise of 1850—both of which ensured that slave and free states were admitted to the Union in equal numbers—cooled but did end sectional hatred.

LAST-DITCH EFFORTS. Congress met in 1860 under the most difficult of circumstances: Southern states were threatening to secede, or leave, the Union, and though Northerners wanted to avoid civil war, they were only willing to go so far in seeking compromise solutions. In this tense atmosphere Congress considered hundreds of amendments, but opened debate on only a few. An amendment offered by John J. Crittenden of Kentucky would have allowed slavery south of the Missouri Compromise line and outlawed it north of the line, and would have counted a slave as three–fifths of a person when determining representation. This alone might have worked, but the Crittenden amendment also declared that these provisions were not amendable and that Congress could never alter the Constitution to abolish slavery. Like many others, this amendment failed. Early in 1861 a "Peace Conference" called by several states attempted to offer its own amendments, but these, too, were quickly discarded.

Finally, in February 1861, Thomas Corwin of Ohio offered an amendment proposal that satisfied Congress. The Corwin amendment proposal read:

> **No amendment shall be made to the Constitution which will authorize or give to Congress the power to abolish or interfere, within any State, with the domestic institutions thereof, including that of persons held to labor or service by the laws of said State.**

The amendment was approved in the House by a vote of 133 to 65, and in the Senate on March 3, 1861, by a vote of 24 to 12, but the fact that many Southern members of the Congress had returned to their states undermined the vote. The amendment had the support of President Lincoln, but only two states, Ohio and Maryland, ratified this proposed amendment.

In the end, constitutional amendment did not settle the slavery question—war did. Seven Southern states seceded from the Union by February 1, 1861, and on April 13 of that year Confederate troops began shelling the Union's Fort Sumter in South Carolina. For four years Union and Confederate troops fought a bitter Civil War to decide the issues that Congress had tried unsuccessfully to resolve. Only when the South had been defeated militarily was the nation able to pass two amendments—the Fourteenth and the Fifteenth—that put an end to the evil institution of slavery and gave blacks the right to vote.

Protecting Children

Throughout the early part of American history children as young as seven or eight regularly worked both in and outside the home to help

Amendment
Proposals

The Child Labor Amendment of 1924 was passed by both the House and the Senate, but stalled out in the process of being ratified by the states. Courtesy of the Library of Congress.

A BALANCED BUDGET AMENDMENT

Though politicians throughout American history have expressed concern with allowing the government to borrow money to finance its activities, it was not until the twentieth century that the question of a balanced federal budget became an important political issue. During the 1930s, federal spending on social programs grew dramatically. President Franklin Delano Roosevelt's New Deal programs sought to ease the effects of the Great Depression by borrowing money to fund programs that provided work and assistance for many Americans. The federal government was spending more than it was raising in taxes and revenues, leading to a budget deficit (the difference between spending and revenues). Opponents of maintaining a federal budget deficit began to suggest that what was needed to curb government spending was an amendment calling for a balanced federal budget.

During the 1980s and 1990s the federal budget deficit grew dramatically, and so did interest in a balanced budget amendment. Beginning in 1981 a series of amendments began to be debated in Congress. Though these amendments varied in their details, most required that

support their families. Many boys left home to apprentice in a trade between the ages of ten and fourteen, and girls often performed household work. As large companies emerged in the nineteenth century, however, more and more children began to work in factories, textile mills, and mines. Many of these jobs exposed children to dangerous working conditions and long hours. By the late nineteenth century, reformers began to urge that children remain in school and that they be protected from working long hours in dangerous jobs. These reformers began a movement that culminated in the Child Labor Amendment of 1924.

The National Child Labor Committee (NCLC), formed in April 1904, became the leader in the campaign to reform working conditions for children. The NCLC was alarmed by the number of children who worked. By 1900 it was estimated that 1.75 million children under the age of fifteen held jobs. Twenty–five percent of the employees of Southern cotton mills were under fifteen, and half of these employees were younger than twelve. The NCLC publicized the problems of child labor and pushed for laws that would protect children. The first federal child

the president submit a balanced budget to Congress and stated that Congress could approve an unbalanced budget only with the approval of three–fifths of the Congress. Most amendments included provisions that allowed for unbalanced budgets in time of war. Such amendments came near passage in 1982 and again in 1994, when House Republicans promoted a set of proposals for government reform they called their "Contract with America."

Many Americans supported the idea of a balanced budget amendment because it seemed like a good, common sense rule. Most households could not survive by spending more than they earned, so why should the federal government be allowed to? But constitutional scholars and economists voiced strong objections to such amendments. Economists objected that the amendment would not allow the president and Congress the flexibility they needed to react to economic change. Constitutional scholars worried that the amendment would bring the courts into the budget-making process in ways that would damage the functioning of government. With the amendment's repeated failure in Congress and the substantial reduction of the federal debt in the late 1990s the balanced budget amendment disappeared from public debate.

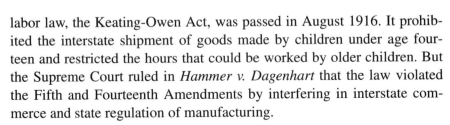

labor law, the Keating-Owen Act, was passed in August 1916. It prohibited the interstate shipment of goods made by children under age fourteen and restricted the hours that could be worked by older children. But the Supreme Court ruled in *Hammer v. Dagenhart* that the law violated the Fifth and Fourteenth Amendments by interfering in interstate commerce and state regulation of manufacturing.

Though some child labor reformers called for a constitutional amendment, the NCLC continued to push for legislation. In response to the Supreme Court's *Hammer v. Dagenhart* ruling, Congress revised the Revenue Act of 1919 to impose a tax on any profits arising from child labor. The textile industry opposed the law and took their case to the Supreme Court. In *Bailey v. Drexel Furniture Company,* the Court again struck down a child labor law, this time ruling that the tax on child labor was actually a penalty and thus violated the Tenth Amendment.

With this second Supreme Court defeat the NCLC realized that a constitutional amendment was the best way to achieve its goals. But, according to some historians, the time for passing such an amendment

Amendment Proposals

had passed. Between 1913 and 1920 Americans had passed more amendments than in any comparable period since the passage of the Bill of Rights. Amendments were widely seen as effective instruments for achieving social change. But as the Eighteenth Amendment, which banned the sale, manufacture, and distribution of alcohol, came to be so widely disliked and disregarded in the 1920s, public opinion began to turn against using amendments to fix social problems.

The following Child Labor Amendment was presented to Congress in the spring of 1924:

> **Section 1. The Congress shall have the power to limit, regulate, and prohibit the labor of persons under eighteen years of age.**
>
> **Section 2. The power of the several States is unimpaired by this article except that the operation of State laws shall be suspended to the extent necessary to give effect to the legislation enacted by the Congress.**

The amendment passed in the House on April 26, 1924, by a vote of 297-69 and in the Senate on June 2, 1924, by a vote of 61-23, and was sent to the states for ratification following the Senate vote. Supporters expected speedy ratification, but soon found that the amendment faced serious opposition. Farmers feared that the amendment would keep children from working on family farms; newspapers feared that they would lose their delivery boys. The Roman Catholic church called the amendment a Communist program. Many conservative groups labeled the amendment another attempt by the federal government to control people's lives. In a reflection of the political climate, the first three states to vote on the amendment rejected it. By 1925 only three states had ratified the amendment, while thirteen states had rejected it. Ratification would be impossible unless one of the states changed its vote.

Efforts at securing ratification continued throughout the 1930s. Fourteen more states voted for ratification in 1933 alone, and by 1938 a total of twenty–eight states supported the amendment. But this was still not enough. In the meantime, the federal government became increasingly active in its regulation of child labor. The Fair Labor Standards Act of 1938 provided minimum working ages for many dangerous jobs, but allowed children under age sixteen to work in certain jobs such as in farming, as newsboys, and in industries not engaged in interstate commerce. This legislation pleased both sides, and the Supreme Court offered its stamp of approval with its ruling in *U.S. v. Darby* (1941). The Child Labor Amendment was dead, but its goal—protecting children—had largely been achieved.

More Rights for Women

The passage of the Nineteenth Amendment had granted women their long-sought right to vote, but advocates of women's rights knew that it came nowhere near granting women full equality. What was needed,

Some women were not in support of the Equal Rights Amendment, fearing that women needed to be protected from working long hours at dangerous jobs.

Reproduced by permission of AP/Wide World Photos.

Amendment Proposals

claimed Alice Paul, founder of the National Women's Party, was an amendment that declared the legal equality of men and women. She proposed the following Equal Rights Amendment in 1923: "Men and women shall have equal rights throughout the United States and in every place subject to its jurisdiction. Congress shall have power to enforce this article by appropriate legislation." This amendment was regularly submitted to Congress for the next twenty years, but not until 1972 did Congress send an approved version of the Equal Rights Amendment (ERA) to the states.

The years leading up to Congressional approval of the ERA saw a pitched battle between those who wanted equality for women and those who believed women needed protection. The Supreme Court, in 1908, had ruled for protection in *Muller v. Oregon,* arguing that "the difference between the sexes ... justif[ies] a different rule respecting a restriction of the hours of labor," and approved of the idea that a woman's "physical stature" should keep her from performing certain jobs. Proponents of protection argued that women needed to be protected from working long hours and dangerous jobs, and they worried that declaring women equal would allow such problems as women serving in the military. Proponents of equality, on the other hand, argued that a constitutional amendment was necessary to give women equal access to jobs and to ensure that women would not be passed over for promotions on the basis of their sex. Resistance to an ERA from powerful protectionists—including President John F. Kennedy and former first lady Eleanor Roosevelt—kept the amendment from gaining Congressional approval through the 1960s.

Beginning in the 1960s, however, popular attitudes toward women began to change in ways that made it seem more likely that an ERA could succeed. The 1963 publication of Betty Friedan's *The Feminine Mystique*, which revealed the deep dissatisfaction of American housewives, helped spark the modern feminist movement. With others, Friedan helped form the National Organization for Women (NOW). Adopting tactics like those used by civil rights groups that worked to ensure equal rights for African Americans, NOW campaigned for equal opportunities for women in education, employment, and politics. With resistance to the ERA finally disappearing, the House voted 354 to 23 for the amendment on October 12, 1971, and the Senate approved it 84 to 8 on March 22, 1972. On the latter date the Equal Rights Amendment was sent to the states for ratification, with the provision that it must be approved within seven years.

*Gloria Steinem
campaigned along
with the National
Organization for
Women (NOW) for
equal opportunities
for women.* Reproduced
by permission of AP/Wide
World Photos.

CONSERVATIVE RESISTANCE. The ERA enjoyed a brief flush of success, as
thirty states ratified the amendment within a year of its passage in Congress. But a backlash led by conservative groups meant that the ERA
never received the remaining eight votes it needed for ratification. The
Supreme Court's 1973 *Roe v. Wade* ruling, which upheld a woman's right
to an abortion, alarmed those who feared that the expansion of women's
rights would endanger the family structure. Conservative leader Phyllis
Schlafly of the National Committee to STOP ERA inflamed public opinion by suggesting that women would be abandoning their families to

**Amendment
Proposals**

*Supporters of the
ERA were surprised
by the organized
resistance to the
amendment.* Reproduced
by permission of the Corbis
Corporation (Bellevue).

work long hours and serve in the military. Other ERA opponents scared people with images of same-sex bathrooms and homosexual marriage.

This organized resistance to the ERA, which caught supporters by surprise, led several states to rescind (withdraw) their ratification. As the seven-year deadline for ratification neared the amendment was still three states short of approval. After a difficult political battle ERA supporters convinced Congress to grant an extension of the ratification deadline. Yet even the extension did not help, for by June 30, 1982, the ERA remained three votes shy of approval. Efforts to reintroduce the amendment in Congress since have all failed.

As with the Child Labor Amendment, however, the social and political changes that allowed Congressional passage of the ERA made actual ratification of the amendment seem unnecessary. By the 1970s, legislation and judicial decisions had granted women many of the rights that the amendment would have secured. Title VII of the Civil Rights Act of 1964 prohibited employment discrimination based upon sex, and Title IX of the Education Amendments of 1972 made federal financial assistance for educational institutions contingent upon their offering equal opportunities for women. The latter act is largely responsible for the creation of

women's athletics programs in colleges. Other acts banned significant forms of sex-based discrimination. And in a series of cases the Supreme Court reversed its earlier stance concerning the "protection" of women. So, while the Equal Rights Amendment was not ratified, women enjoyed most of the advantages that it would have bestowed.

Solving Problems by Amendment: The Failures

Amendments to the Constitution offer Americans one of the most decisive ways of reshaping the direction of their government. Over the country's first two hundred years, twenty–seven amendments have been added to the Constitution. Those amendments now help determine such things as the rights individuals retain, who can vote and how those votes translate to representation, and how our elected officials will succeed one another and be paid. Even the unratified amendments have exerted a real influence on the shape of civic life. The push for protecting children in the workplace led to laws offering protections, and the quest for the Equal Rights Amendment helped spark legislation that granted equal opportunities for women.

Congress has been offered over 11,000 amendments in the course of its history, yet only 33 have ever been approved by Congress and sent to the states. What has happened to the rest? Many are referred to Congressional committees and are never heard from again; many others are quietly voted upon and rejected. But an important minority of potential and proposed amendments have appeared before Congress again and again, and have generated real public interest. Even though they have not been approved, proposed amendments on such topics as electoral college reform, a balanced federal budget, flag desecration, abortion, and congressional term limits continue to engage policy makers and politicians. Do the following proposals stand any chance at becoming amendments?

ELECTORAL COLLEGE REFORM. Among the most frequently proposed amendments are those encouraging the reform of the electoral college, a complicated system used to elect the president and vice-president. Under the system, voters cast their votes for electors and not the candidates themselves. States are given a number of electors equal to their representation in Congress, and these electors meet to cast their votes for president and vice-president. The system has sometimes led to strange outcomes: in 1888, for example, Grover Cleveland received 100,000 more popular votes than Benjamin Harrison but Harrison was elected president by the electoral college. Similar problems marred the elections of 1824, 1876, 1960, and 2000.

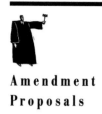

Amendment Proposals

THE LAST UNRATIFIED AMENDMENT: D.C. STATEHOOD

An amendment referred to the states for ratification in 1978 attempted to solve the nearly 200-year-old problem of whether residents of the District of Columbia should have representation in Congress. Article I, Section 8 of the Constitution, which granted Congress the power to create a district that would serve as the seat of the federal government, allowed for the creation of the District of Columbia on a large plot of land granted to the federal government by the states of Maryland and Virginia. The problem, however, was that the citizens of the district had no one in Congress to represent their viewpoint.

Over the years Congress experimented with different ways of governing the district. Throughout the nineteenth and into the mid-twentieth century the district was subject to the whims of Congress for its governance. At times the district's citizens were authorized to elect a mayor, while at other times Congress appointed a mayor or a board of commissioners to run the district. In the 1960s, however, things began to change. The Twenty–third Amendment, passed in 1961, gave district residents the right to vote in presidential elections, and in 1970 Congress authorized the election of a non-voting delegate to the House of Representatives. But residents of the district insisted that these measures did not go far enough. The district had grown dramatically in size over the years, and had more than 750,000 residents in 1960. In the climate of growing concern for equal representation for all people that characterized the 1960s it seemed odd that so many Americans should lack representation simply because they lived in the nation's capitol. The problem was compounded by the fact that the district's population was largely black, yet the district was ruled by conservative and even racist Southern senators who ignored the population's needs.

After a significant period of debate during which a variety of solutions to the problem were discussed (including giving the lands in the

Congress has received more than 850 proposals for reform of the electoral college. Two such reforms have been adopted in the Twelfth and Twenty–third Amendments, but calls for more reform have occurred throughout U.S. history. The most popular of the proposed

district back to Maryland and Virginia and allowing residents to vote as citizens of those states), Congress approved the following amendment by a vote of 289 to 127 in the House and 67 to 32 in the Senate:

Section 1. For purposes of representation in the Congress, election of the President and Vice President, and article V of this Constitution, the District constituting the seat of government of the United States shall be treated as though it were a State.

Section 2. The exercise of the rights and powers conferred under this article shall be done by the people of the District constituting the seat of government, and as shall be provided by the Congress.

Section 3. The twenty–third article of amendment to the Constitution of the United States is hereby repealed.

Section 4. This article shall be inoperative, unless it shall have been ratified as an amendment to the Constitution by the legislatures of three–fourths of the several States within seven years from the date of its submission.

Though residents of the district greeted the Congressional approval of the amendment with enthusiasm, that enthusiasm was not widely shared by the states. Some amendment opponents said that ratification would have to be unanimous, for Article V of the Constitution held that "no state without its consent shall be deprived of its equal suffrage in the Senate." (Voting for the amendment meant that each state's share of power in the Senate would be reduced slightly.) Republican opponents predicted that the largely black population of the district would elect two Democratic senators and one Democratic representative. They resisted this challenge to the balance of power. By the end of the seven year ratification deadline in 1985 only sixteen states had ratified the amendment; the remainder of the states had either rejected it or simply ignored it. The citizens of the District of Columbia still remain without adequate representation at the federal level.

amendments calls for direct popular election of candidates. This would be the most democratic method, ensuring that the will of the people would be most clearly heard. Other reforms call for appointing electors to individual districts within states, for dividing electors according to

Amendment Proposals

the popular vote within the states, or for giving all of a state's votes to the candidate who won the popular vote within the state. The extraordinarily narrow margins by which presidential candidates won individual states in the 2000 election prompted renewed interest in reforming election procedures.

FLAG DESECRATION. Legal protections for the American flag have long been popular with patriotic Americans. At the turn of the twentieth century most states had laws that banned improper use of the flag (for advertising, for example) and flag desecration (which included both destroying and defaming the flag). For a time the Supreme Court backed such laws, finding it reasonable that states should wish to encourage patriotism. Though a 1943 ruling in the case of *West Virginia Board of Education v. Barnette* established that students could not be forced to salute the flag, actual flag desecration remained off limits—until 1989. That year, in the *Texas v. Johnson* decision concerning a Texas man who had burned a flag in protest, the Court ruled that "the government may not prohibit expression simply because it disagrees with its message." This ruling, which declared that destroying the flag was an act of expression protected by the First Amendment, made flag desecration the hot political issue of the day and led to calls for the creation of an amendment offering protection for the flag.

A flag desecration amendment posed difficult problems for politicians. No one in public office could afford to come out in favor of flag burning, yet an amendment seemed too extreme a limit of people's expression. When a proposed amendment that stated "The Congress and the States shall have power to prohibit the physical desecration of the flag of the United States" was voted down fifty–one to forty–eight in October 1989, lawmakers instead passed the Flag Protection Act. No sooner had the act been passed than protesters staged flag burnings to bring the law before the Supreme Court. In the case of *United States v. Eichman,* the Court ruled that the law was unconstitutional because it banned expression protected by the First Amendment. This ruling again inflamed public opinion, but renewed attempts to pass an amendment were twice narrowly defeated by Congress and the call for such an amendment quietly died. Historian Alan Brinkley wrote, however, that "Democracies secure in their identities and confident of their principles ... do not usually feel the need to define patriotism by law. But given the conspicuous absence of either security or confidence in contemporary American culture, no one should assume that the flag issue has been put to rest for good."

ABORTION. The 1973 *Roe v. Wade* Supreme Court ruling protecting a woman's right to an abortion encouraged a variety of efforts to overturn the ruling with a constitutional amendment. Generally supported by Republicans and religious conservatives, these amendment proposals sought to protect unborn babies in a variety of ways. Some proposals wanted to define a fetus (unborn baby) as a person from the moment of conception and thus give the fetus all the protections of any person; others proposed to protect life at all stages of development; and still others wanted to leave decisions about abortion up to individual states. Despite their support by Republican politicians no such amendment has ever come close to passage in Congress. Anti-abortion advocates have instead been forced to pursue their agenda through legislation and the hope that the Supreme Court will eventually overturn the *Roe v. Wade* decision.

CONGRESSIONAL TERM LIMITS. One of the hottest political issues of the 1990s was congressional term limits, the attempt to limit the number of times that an elected official could be returned to office. Term limits were quite popular with Americans who came to believe that many legislators were more responsive to special interests (such as lobbying groups funded by corporations) than they were to voters' needs. Term limits,

Amendment Proposals

One proposed amendment wanted to define when an unborn baby is a person. Reproduced by permission of AP/Wide World Photos.

said its backers, would remove career politicians and allow ordinary citizens to run for office. Opponents of term limits argued that many legislators became more effective as they served in office longer, and that voters already had the right to turn out of office anyone they disliked.

During the 1994 congressional elections, the Republican party supported a set of proposals for government reform, the "Contract with America," that included a call for a constitutional amendment to limit the terms of members of Congress. After considerable debate the House soundly defeated such an amendment on March 29, 1995. Several states created their own term limit laws, but those that reached the Supreme Court were quickly overturned. In the end, a term limit amendment seemed an unnecessary adjustment to a system that worked fairly well.

Conclusion

Will the Constitution be amended again? History assures us that it most certainly will—whenever a majority of Americans and their representatives feel that their needs can only be addressed by a constitutional amendment. Constitutional scholar Richard B. Bernstein argues that the history of those amendments that have been proposed but not ratified points to "an important principle at the heart of the amending process: a successful amendment campaign requires a sustained consensus that a problem exists which is not readily fixed by anything short of an amendment." Amendments are decisive and powerful; they indicate that a policy is so central to our conception of government that we are willing to enshrine it in our most sacred civic document. That the United States Constitution is flexible enough to permit such adjustment offers unique proof of its success.

For More Information

Books

Ames, Herman V. *The Proposed Amendments to the Constitution of the United States during the First Century of its History,* in *Annual Report of the American Historical Association for the Year 1896,* Vol. 2. Washington, D.C.: Government Printing Office, 1897.

Bernstein, Richard B., with Jerome Agel. *Amending America: If We Love the Constitution So Much, Why Do We Keep Trying to Change It?* New York: Times Books, 1993.

Curtis, Michael Kent, editor. *The Constitution and the Flag: The Flag Burning Cases.* 2 Vols. New York and London: Garland Publishing, 1993.

Goldstein, Robert Justin. *Saving "Old Glory": The History of the American Flag Desecration Controversy.* Boulder, Colorado, San Francisco, and Oxford: Westview Press, 1995.

Goldstein, Robert Justin, ed. *Desecrating the American Flag.* Syracuse, New York: Syracuse University Press, 1996.

Kyvig, David E. *Explicit and Authentic Acts: Amending the U.S. Constitution, 1776-1995.* Lawrence: University of Press of Kansas, 1996.

Levy, Leonard W., Kenneth L. Karst, Dennis J. Mahoney, and John G. West, Jr., eds. *Encyclopedia of the American Constitution.* New York: Macmillan, 1986 and 1992 supp.

Lieberman, Jethro K. *Evolving Constitution: How the Supreme Court Has Ruled on Issues from Abortion to Zoning.* New York: Random House, 1992.

Palmer, Kris E., editor. *Constitutional Amendments, 1789 to the Present.* Detroit: Gale Group, 2000.

Vile, John R. *Contemporary Questions Surrounding the Constitutional Amending Process.* Westport, Connecticut: Praeger, 1993.

Vile, John R. *Encyclopedia of Constitutional Amendments, Proposed Amendments, and Amending Issues, 1789-1995.* Santa Barbara, California: ABC-CLIO, 1996.

Vile, John R. *Rewriting the United States Constitution: An Examination of Proposals from Reconstruction to the Present.* Westport, Connecticut: Praeger, 1991.

Articles

Brinkley, Alan. "Old Glory: The Saga of a National Love Affair," *New York Times,* July 1, 1990, sec. 4, p. 2.

Web Sites

"Amendments Never Ratified for the U.S. Constitution." [Online] http://www.law.emory.edu/pub-cgi/print_hit_bold.pl/ FEDERAL/usconst/notamend.html (accessed August 1, 2000).

**Amendment
Proposals**

"Chronology of the Equal Rights Amendment 1923-1996." [Online] http://now.org/issues/economic/cea/history.html (accessed August 1, 2000.)

"The U.S. Constitution Online." [Online] http:/www.usconstitution.net/constnot.html (accessed August 1, 2000).

Constitution of the United States of America

We the People of the United States, in Order to form a more perfect Union, establish Justice, insure domestic Tranquility, provide for the common defense, promote the general Welfare, and secure the Blessings of Liberty to ourselves and our Posterity, do ordain and establish this Constitution for the United States of America.

Article I

Items in italic have since been amended or superseded.
A portion of Article I, Section 2, was modified by Section 2 of the Fourteenth Amendment; Article I, Section 3, was modified by the Seventeenth Amendment; Article I, Section 4, was modified by Section 2 of the Twentieth Amendment; and Article I, Section 9, was modified by the Sixteenth Amendment.

Section 1.

All legislative Powers herein granted shall be vested in a Congress of the United States, which shall consist of a Senate and House of Representatives.

Section 2.

The House of Representatives shall be composed of Members chosen every second Year by the People of the several States, and the Electors in each State shall have the Qualifications requisite for Electors of the most numerous Branch of the State Legislature.

No Person shall be a Representative who shall not have attained to the Age of twenty five Years, and been seven Years a Citizen of the

Constitution of the United States of America

United States, and who shall not, when elected, be an Inhabitant of that State in which he shall be chosen.

Representatives and direct Taxes shall be apportioned among the several States which may be included within this Union, according to their respective Numbers, which shall be determined by adding to the whole Number of free Persons, including those bound to Service for a Term of Years, and excluding Indians not taxed, three fifths of all other Persons. The actual Enumeration shall be made within three Years after the first Meeting of the Congress of the United States, and within every subsequent Term of ten Years, in such Manner as they shall by Law direct. The Number of Representatives shall not exceed one for every thirty Thousand, but each State shall have at Least one Representative; and until such enumeration shall be made, the State of New Hampshire shall be entitled to chuse three, Massachusetts eight, Rhode-Island and Providence Plantations one, Connecticut five, New-York six, New Jersey four, Pennsylvania eight, Delaware one, Maryland six, Virginia ten, North Carolina five, South Carolina five, and Georgia three.

When vacancies happen in the Representation from any State, the Executive Authority thereof shall issue Writs of Election to fill such Vacancies.

The House of Representatives shall chuse their Speaker and other Officers; and shall have the sole Power of Impeachment.

Section 3.

The Senate of the United States shall be composed of two Senators from each State, *chosen by the Legislature thereof* for six Years; and each Senator shall have one Vote.

Immediately after they shall be assembled in Consequence of the first Election, they shall be divided as equally as may be into three Classes. The Seats of the Senators of the first Class shall be vacated at the Expiration of the second Year, of the second Class at the Expiration of the fourth Year, and of the third Class at the Expiration of the sixth Year, so that one third may be chosen every second Year; *and if Vacancies happen by Resignation, or otherwise, during the Recess of the Legislature of any State, the Executive thereof may make temporary Appointments until the next Meeting of the Legislature, which shall then fill such Vacancies.*

No Person shall be a Senator who shall not have attained to the Age of thirty Years, and been nine Years a Citizen of the United States, and who shall not, when elected, be an Inhabitant of that State for which he shall be chosen.

The Vice President of the United States shall be President of the Senate, but shall have no Vote, unless they be equally divided.

The Senate shall chuse their other Officers, and also a President pro tempore, in the Absence of the Vice President, or when he shall exercise the Office of President of the United States.

The Senate shall have the sole Power to try all Impeachments. When sitting for that Purpose, they shall be on Oath or Affirmation. When the President of the United States is tried, the Chief Justice shall preside: And no Person shall be convicted without the Concurrence of two thirds of the Members present.

Judgment in Cases of Impeachment shall not extend further than to removal from Office, and disqualification to hold and enjoy any Office of honor, Trust or Profit under the United States: but the Party convicted shall nevertheless be liable and subject to Indictment, Trial, Judgment and Punishment, according to Law.

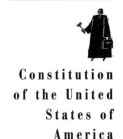

Section 4.

The Times, Places and Manner of holding Elections for Senators and Representatives, shall be prescribed in each State by the Legislature thereof; but the Congress may at any time by Law make or alter such Regulations, except as to the Places of chusing Senators.

The Congress shall assemble at least once in every Year, and such Meeting shall *be on the first Monday in December,* unless they shall by Law appoint a different Day.

Section 5.

Each House shall be the Judge of the Elections, Returns and Qualifications of its own Members, and a Majority of each shall constitute a Quorum to do Business; but a smaller Number may adjourn from day to day, and may be authorized to compel the Attendance of absent Members, in such Manner, and under such Penalties as each House may provide.

Each House may determine the Rules of its Proceedings, punish its Members for disorderly Behaviour, and, with the Concurrence of two thirds, expel a Member.

Each House shall keep a Journal of its Proceedings, and from time to time publish the same, excepting such Parts as may in their Judgment

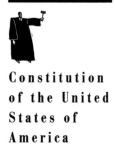

require Secrecy; and the Yeas and Nays of the Members of either House on any question shall, at the Desire of one fifth of those Present, be entered on the Journal.

Neither House, during the Session of Congress, shall, without the Consent of the other, adjourn for more than three days, nor to any other Place than that in which the two Houses shall be sitting.

Section 6.

The Senators and Representatives shall receive a Compensation for their Services, to be ascertained by Law, and paid out of the Treasury of the United States. They shall in all Cases, except Treason, Felony and Breach of the Peace, be privileged from Arrest during their Attendance at the Session of their respective Houses, and in going to and returning from the same; and for any Speech or Debate in either House, they shall not be questioned in any other Place.

No Senator or Representative shall, during the Time for which he was elected, be appointed to any civil Office under the Authority of the United States, which shall have been created, or the Emoluments where-of shall have been encreased during such time; and no Person holding any Office under the United States, shall be a Member of either House during his Continuance in Office.

Section 7.

All Bills for raising Revenue shall originate in the House of Representatives; but the Senate may propose or concur with Amendments as on other Bills.

Every Bill which shall have passed the House of Representatives and the Senate, shall, before it become a Law, be presented to the President of the United States: If he approve he shall sign it, but if not he shall return it, with his Objections to that House in which it shall have originated, who shall enter the Objections at large on their Journal, and proceed to reconsider it. If after such Reconsideration two thirds of that House shall agree to pass the Bill, it shall be sent, together with the Objections, to the other House, by which it shall likewise be reconsidered, and if approved by two thirds of that House, it shall become a Law. But in all such Cases the Votes of both Houses shall be determined by yeas and Nays, and the Names of the Persons voting for and against the Bill shall be entered on the Journal of each House respectively. If any Bill shall not be returned by the President within ten Days (Sundays excepted) after it shall have been presented to him, the Same shall be a Law, in like Manner as if he had signed it, unless the Congress by their Adjournment prevent its Return, in which Case it shall not be a Law.

Every Order, Resolution, or Vote to which the Concurrence of the Senate and House of Representatives may be necessary (except on a question of Adjournment) shall be presented to the President of the United States; and before the Same shall take Effect, shall be approved by him, or being disapproved by him, shall be repassed by two thirds of the Senate and House of Representatives, according to the Rules and Limitations prescribed in the Case of a Bill.

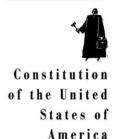

Section 8.

The Congress shall have Power To lay and collect Taxes, Duties, Imposts and Excises, to pay the Debts and provide for the common Defence and general Welfare of the United States; but all Duties, Imposts and Excises shall be uniform throughout the United States;

To borrow Money on the credit of the United States;

To regulate Commerce with foreign Nations, and among the several States, and with the Indian Tribes;

To establish an uniform Rule of Naturalization, and uniform Laws on the subject of Bankruptcies throughout the United States;

To coin Money, regulate the Value thereof, and of foreign Coin, and fix the Standard of Weights and Measures;

To provide for the Punishment of counterfeiting the Securities and current Coin of the United States;

To establish Post Offices and post Roads;

To promote the Progress of Science and useful Arts, by securing for limited Times to Authors and Inventors the exclusive Right to their respective Writings and Discoveries;

To constitute Tribunals inferior to the supreme Court;

To define and punish Piracies and Felonies committed on the high Seas, and Offences against the Law of Nations;

To declare War, grant Letters of Marque and Reprisal, and make Rules concerning Captures on Land and Water;

To raise and support Armies, but no Appropriation of Money to that Use shall be for a longer Term than two Years;

Constitution of the United States of America

To provide and maintain a Navy;

To make Rules for the Government and Regulation of the land and naval Forces;

To provide for calling forth the Militia to execute the Laws of the Union, suppress Insurrections and repel Invasions;

To provide for organizing, arming, and disciplining, the Militia, and for governing such Part of them as may be employed in the Service of the United States, reserving to the States respectively, the Appointment of the Officers, and the Authority of training the Militia according to the discipline prescribed by Congress;

To exercise exclusive Legislation in all Cases whatsoever, over such District (not exceeding ten Miles square) as may, by Cession of particular States, and the Acceptance of Congress, become the Seat of the Government of the United States, and to exercise like Authority over all Places purchased by the Consent of the Legislature of the State in which the Same shall be, for the Erection of Forts, Magazines, Arsenals, dock-Yards, and other needful Buildings;—And

To make all Laws which shall be necessary and proper for carrying into Execution the foregoing Powers, and all other Powers vested by this Constitution in the Government of the United States, or in any Department or Officer thereof.

Section 9.

The Migration or Importation of such Persons as any of the States now existing shall think proper to admit, shall not be prohibited by the Congress prior to the Year one thousand eight hundred and eight, but a Tax or duty may be imposed on such Importation, not exceeding ten dollars for each Person.

The Privilege of the Writ of Habeas Corpus shall not be suspended, unless when in Cases of Rebellion or Invasion the public Safety may require it.

No Bill of Attainder or ex post facto Law shall be passed.

No Capitation, or other direct, Tax shall be laid, *unless in Proportion to the Census or enumeration herein before directed to be taken.*

No Tax or Duty shall be laid on Articles exported from any State.

No Preference shall be given by any Regulation of Commerce or Revenue to the Ports of one State over those of another; nor shall

Vessels bound to, or from, one State, be obliged to enter, clear, or pay Duties in another.

No Money shall be drawn from the Treasury, but in Consequence of Appropriations made by Law; and a regular Statement and Account of the Receipts and Expenditures of all public Money shall be published from time to time.

No Title of Nobility shall be granted by the United States: And no Person holding any Office of Profit or Trust under them, shall, without the Consent of the Congress, accept of any present, Emolument, Office, or Title, of any kind whatever, from any King, Prince, or foreign State.

Section 10.

No State shall enter into any Treaty, Alliance, or Confederation; grant Letters of Marque and Reprisal; coin Money; emit Bills of Credit; make any Thing but gold and silver Coin a Tender in Payment of Debts; pass any Bill of Attainder, ex post facto Law, or Law impairing the Obligation of Contracts, or grant any Title of Nobility.

No State shall, without the Consent of the Congress, lay any Imposts or Duties on Imports or Exports, except what may be absolutely necessary for executing it's inspection Laws: and the net Produce of all Duties and Imposts, laid by any State on Imports or Exports, shall be for the Use of the Treasury of the United States; and all such Laws shall be subject to the Revision and Controul of the Congress.

No State shall, without the Consent of Congress, lay any Duty of Tonnage, keep Troops, or Ships of War in time of Peace, enter into any Agreement or Compact with another State, or with a foreign Power, or engage in War, unless actually invaded, or in such imminent Danger as will not admit of delay.

Article II

Article II, Section 1, was superseded by the Twelfth Amendment
Article II, Section 1, was modified by the Twenty-fifth Amendment.

Section 1.

The executive Power shall be vested in a President of the United States of America. He shall hold his Office during the Term of four Years, and, together with the Vice President, chosen for the same Term, be elected, as follows:

Constitution of the United States of America

Each State shall appoint, in such Manner as the Legislature thereof may direct, a Number of Electors, equal to the whole Number of Senators and Representatives to which the State may be entitled in the Congress: but no Senator or Representative, or Person holding an Office of Trust or Profit under the United States, shall be appointed an Elector.

The Electors shall meet in their respective States, and vote by Ballot for two Persons, of whom one at least shall not be an Inhabitant of the same State with themselves. And they shall make a List of all the Persons voted for, and of the Number of Votes for each; which List they shall sign and certify, and transmit sealed to the Seat of the Government of the United States, directed to the President of the Senate. The President of the Senate shall, in the Presence of the Senate and House of Representatives, open all the Certificates, and the Votes shall then be counted. The Person having the greatest Number of Votes shall be the President, if such Number be a Majority of the whole Number of Electors appointed; and if there be more than one who have such Majority, and have an equal Number of Votes, then the House of Representatives shall immediately chuse by Ballot one of them for President; and if no Person have a Majority, then from the five highest on the List the said House shall in like Manner chuse the President. But in chusing the President, the Votes shall be taken by States, the Representation from each State having one Vote; A quorum for this purpose shall consist of a Member or Members from two thirds of the States, and a Majority of all the States shall be necessary to a Choice. In every Case, after the Choice of the President, the Person having the greatest Number of Votes of the Electors shall be the Vice President. But if there should remain two or more who have equal Votes, the Senate shall chuse from them by Ballot the Vice President.

The Congress may determine the Time of chusing the Electors, and the Day on which they shall give their Votes; which Day shall be the same throughout the United States.

No Person except a natural born Citizen, or a Citizen of the United States, at the time of the Adoption of this Constitution, shall be eligible to the Office of President; neither shall any Person be eligible to that Office who shall not have attained to the Age of thirty five Years, and been fourteen Years a Resident within the United States.

In Case of the Removal of the President from Office, or of his Death, Resignation, or Inability to discharge the Powers and Duties of the said Office, the Same shall devolve on the Vice President, and the Congress may by Law provide for the Case of Removal, Death, Resignation or

Inability, both of the President and Vice President, declaring what Officer shall then act as President, and such Officer shall act accordingly, until the Disability be removed, or a President shall be elected.

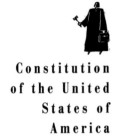

The President shall, at stated Times, receive for his Services, a Compensation, which shall neither be increased nor diminished during the Period for which he shall have been elected, and he shall not receive within that Period any other Emolument from the United States, or any of them.

Before he enter on the Execution of his Office, he shall take the following Oath or Affirmation:—"I do solemnly swear (or affirm) that I will faithfully execute the Office of President of the United States, and will to the best of my Ability, preserve, protect and defend the Constitution of the United States."

Section 2.

The President shall be Commander in Chief of the Army and Navy of the United States, and of the Militia of the several States, when called into the actual Service of the United States; he may require the Opinion, in writing, of the principal Officer in each of the executive Departments, upon any Subject relating to the Duties of their respective Offices, and he shall have Power to grant Reprieves and Pardons for Offences against the United States, except in Cases of Impeachment. He shall have Power, by and with the Advice and Consent of the Senate, to make Treaties, provided two thirds of the Senators present concur; and he shall nominate, and by and with the Advice and Consent of the Senate, shall appoint Ambassadors, other public Ministers and Consuls, Judges of the supreme Court, and all other Officers of the United States, whose Appointments are not herein otherwise provided for, and which shall be established by Law: but the Congress may by Law vest the Appointment of such inferior Officers, as they think proper, in the President alone, in the Courts of Law, or in the Heads of Departments.

The President shall have Power to fill up all Vacancies that may happen during the Recess of the Senate, by granting Commissions which shall expire at the End of their next Session.

Section 3.

He shall from time to time give to the Congress Information of the State of the Union, and recommend to their Consideration such Measures as he shall judge necessary and expedient; he may, on extraordinary

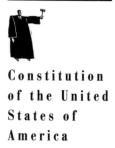

Constitution of the United States of America

Occasions, convene both Houses, or either of them, and in Case of Disagreement between them, with Respect to the Time of Adjournment, he may adjourn them to such Time as he shall think proper; he shall receive Ambassadors and other public Ministers; he shall take Care that the Laws be faithfully executed, and shall Commission all the Officers of the United States.

Section 4.

The President, Vice President and all civil Officers of the United States, shall be removed from Office on Impeachment for, and Conviction of, Treason, Bribery, or other high Crimes and Misdemeanors.

Article III

A portion of Section 2 was modified by the Eleventh Amendment.

Section 1.

The judicial Power of the United States shall be vested in one supreme Court, and in such inferior Courts as the Congress may from time to time ordain and establish. The Judges, both of the supreme and inferior Courts, shall hold their Offices during good Behaviour, and shall, at stated Times, receive for their Services a Compensation, which shall not be diminished during their Continuance in Office.

Section 2.

The judicial Power shall extend to all Cases, in Law and Equity, arising under this Constitution, the Laws of the United States, and Treaties made, or which shall be made, under their Authority;—to all Cases affecting Ambassadors, other public Ministers and Consuls;—to all Cases of admiralty and maritime Jurisdiction;—to Controversies to which the United States shall be a Party; to Controversies between two or more States;—*between a State and Citizens of another State;*—between Citizens of different States; between Citizens of the same State claiming Lands under Grants of different States, and between a State, or the Citizens thereof, and foreign States, Citizens or Subjects.

In all Cases affecting Ambassadors, other public Ministers and Consuls, and those in which a State shall be Party, the supreme Court shall have original Jurisdiction. In all the other Cases before mentioned, the supreme Court shall have appellate Jurisdiction, both as to Law and

Fact, with such Exceptions, and under such Regulations as the Congress shall make.

The Trial of all Crimes, except in Cases of Impeachment, shall be by Jury; and such Trial shall be held in the State where the said Crimes shall have been committed; but when not committed within any State, the Trial shall be at such Place or Places as the Congress may by Law have directed.

Section 3.

Treason against the United States, shall consist only in levying War against them, or in adhering to their Enemies, giving them Aid and Comfort. No Person shall be convicted of Treason unless on the Testimony of two Witnesses to the same overt Act, or on Confession in open Court.

The Congress shall have Power to declare the Punishment of Treason, but no Attainder of Treason shall work Corruption of Blood, or Forfeiture except during the Life of the Person attainted.

Article IV

A portion of Section 2 was superseded by the Thirteenth Amendment.

Section 1.

Full Faith and Credit shall be given in each State to the public Acts, Records, and judicial Proceedings of every other State. And the Congress may by general Laws prescribe the Manner in which such Acts, Records and Proceedings shall be proved, and the Effect thereof.

Section 2.

The Citizens of each State shall be entitled to all Privileges and Immunities of Citizens in the several States.

A Person charged in any State with Treason, Felony, or other Crime, who shall flee from Justice, and be found in another State, shall on Demand of the executive Authority of the State from which he fled, be delivered up, to be removed to the State having Jurisdiction of the Crime.

No Person held to Service or Labour in one State, under the Laws thereof, escaping into another, shall, in Consequence of any Law or Regulation therein, be discharged from such Service or Labour, but shall be delivered up on Claim of the Party to whom such Service or Labour may be due.

Constitution of the United States of America

Section 3.

New States may be admitted by the Congress into this Union; but no new State shall be formed or erected within the Jurisdiction of any other State; nor any State be formed by the Junction of two or more States, or Parts of States, without the Consent of the Legislatures of the States concerned as well as of the Congress.

The Congress shall have Power to dispose of and make all needful Rules and Regulations respecting the Territory or other Property belonging to the United States; and nothing in this Constitution shall be so construed as to Prejudice any Claims of the United States, or of any particular State.

Section 4.

The United States shall guarantee to every State in this Union a Republican Form of Government, and shall protect each of them against Invasion; and on Application of the Legislature, or of the Executive (when the Legislature cannot be convened), against domestic Violence.

Article V

The Congress, whenever two thirds of both Houses shall deem it necessary, shall propose Amendments to this Constitution, or, on the Application of the Legislatures of two thirds of the several States, shall call a Convention for proposing Amendments, which, in either Case, shall be valid to all Intents and Purposes, as Part of this Constitution, when ratified by the Legislatures of three fourths of the several States, or by Conventions in three fourths thereof, as the one or the other Mode of Ratification may be proposed by the Congress; Provided that no Amendment which may be made prior to the Year One thousand eight hundred and eight shall in any Manner affect the first and fourth Clauses in the Ninth Section of the first Article; and that no State, without its Consent, shall be deprived of its equal Suffrage in the Senate.

Article VI

All Debts contracted and Engagements entered into, before the Adoption of this Constitution, shall be as valid against the United States under this Constitution, as under the Confederation.

This Constitution, and the Laws of the United States which shall be made in Pursuance thereof; and all Treaties made, or which shall be made, under the Authority of the United States, shall be the supreme Law of the Land; and the Judges in every State shall be bound thereby, any Thing in the Constitution or Laws of any State to the Contrary notwithstanding.

The Senators and Representatives before mentioned, and the Members of the several State Legislatures, and all executive and judicial Officers, both of the United States and of the several States, shall be bound by Oath or Affirmation, to support this Constitution; but no religious Test shall ever be required as a Qualification to any Office or public Trust under the United States.

Article VII

The Ratification of the Conventions of nine States, shall be sufficient for the Establishment of this Constitution between the States so ratifying the Same.

Attest William Jackson Secretary

Done in Convention by the Unanimous Consent of the States present the Seventeenth Day of September in the Year of our Lord one thousand seven hundred and Eighty seven and of the Independence of the United States of America the Twelfth In witness whereof We have hereunto subscribed our Names,

G° Washington Presidt and deputy from Virginia

Delaware: Geo: Read, Gunning Bedford jun, John Dickinson, Richard Bassett, Jaco: Broom

Maryland: James McHenry, Dan of St Thos. Jenifer, Danl. Carroll

Virginia: John Blair—, James Madison Jr.

North Carolina: Wm. Blount, Richd. Dobbs Spaight, Hu Williamson

South Carolina: J. Rutledge, Charles Cotesworth Pinckney, Charles Pinckney, Pierce Butler

Georgia: William Few, Abr Baldwin

New Hampshire: John Langdon, Nicholas Gilman

Massachusetts: Nathaniel Gorham, Rufus King

Connecticut: Wm. Saml. Johnson Roger Sherman

New York: Alexander Hamilton

**Constitution
of the United
States of
America**

New Jersey: Wil: Livingston, David Brearley, Wm. Paterson, Jona: Dayton

Pennsylvania: B Franklin, Thomas Mifflin, Robt. Morris, Geo. Clymer, Thos. FitzSimons, Jared Ingersoll, James Wilson, Gouv Morris

Index

Index

B

C

Index

Index

I

J

Index

Index

Index

Index